The S & L Insurance Mess: How Did It Happen?

Edward J. Kane

The S & L Insurance Mess: How Did It Happen?

THE URBAN INSTITUTE PRESS
Washington, D.C.

THE URBAN INSTITUTE PRESS
2100 M Street, N.W.
Washington, D.C. 20037

Library of Congress Cataloging in Publication Data

The S & L Insurance Mess: How Did It Happen?/Edward J. Kane
1. Building and loan associations—United States—Government guarantee of deposits. 2. Building and loan associations—United States. 3. Federal Savings and Loan Insurance Corporation.
I. Title. II. Title: S and L Insurance Mess.
HG2151.K35   1989   368.8'54'00973   89-5786

ISBN 0–87766–468–4
ISBN 0–87766–469–2 (casebound)

Printed in the United States of America.

9 8 7 6 5 4 3 2

Distributed by
            University Press of America
4720 Boston Way   3 Henrietta Street
Lanham, MD 20706   London WC2E 8LU ENGLAND

THE URBAN INSTITUTE is a nonprofit policy research and educational organization established in Washington, D.C., in 1968. Its staff investigates the social and economic problems confronting the nation and government policies and programs designed to alleviate such problems. The Institute disseminates significant findings of its research through the publications program of its Press. The Institute has two goals for work in each of its research areas: to help shape thinking about societal problems and efforts to solve them, and to improve government decisions and performance by providing better information and analytic tools.

Through work that ranges from broad conceptual studies to administrative and technical assistance, Institute researchers contribute to the stock of knowledge available to public officials and private individuals and groups concerned with formulating and implementing more efficient and effective government policy.

Conclusions or opinions expressed in Institute Publications are those of the authors and do not necessarily reflect the views of other staff members, officers or trustees of the Institute, advisory groups, or any organizations that provide financial support to the Institute.

To My Children:
Laura, Steve, and Ted

ACKNOWLEDGMENTS

This book was written during a sabbatical leave spent at the Center for Financial System Research in the College of Business of Arizona State University. I am grateful to Ohio State University for giving me leave and to Dean John Kraft and the Center's Director Herbert Kaufman at Arizona State for providing a stimulating and supportive environment in which to work. For additional financial support, I wish to thank the Urban Institute and its sponsors for the study, Citibank, N.A., and the National Corporation for Housing Partnerships.

My perspective on deposit insurance has been shaped by more than a decade of research and teaching on this subject. Looking back over so long a time period, it is impossible for me to identify and thank every economist and policymaker who helped to deepen my understanding of the flaws existing in the current system or to sharpen my analysis of what society should do about them.

Many students and colleagues importantly influenced my evolving views. For hours of enlightening discussion, I wish to thank the members of the Shadow Financial Regulatory Committee and economists who coauthored related studies with me. These coauthors include: Stephen Buser, Andrew Chen, George Benston, Robert Eisenbeis, Paul Horvitz, George Kaufman, Chet Foster, and Haluk Unal.

I also want to thank everyone who contributed directly to the production of this book. Rudolph Penner, George Kaufman, Herbert Kaufman, and Donald Shackelford provided valuable and detailed criticisms of the entire first draft. In addition, Richard Aspinwall, James Croft, Robert Eisenbeis, Kenneth Guenther, Jerry Hawke, Rachel Strauber, and Fred Thompson offered insightful suggestions for strengthening individual chapters. James Barth and Warren Heller furnished me with hard-to-obtain data, which Haluk Unal in part helped me to analyze. Lynn Winkelman typed and retyped the manuscript, while Felicity Skidmore kept the project rolling smoothly and made a series of inspired suggestions for strengthening and clarifying the argument.

As always, my deepest thanks go to my wife, Gloria, for keeping me from wanting to let my work fill up my life.

CONTENTS

Foreword   xvii

**1 Zombie Thrifts and FSLIC: A Federal Ponzi
Scheme?**   1
   The Black Magic of Federal Guarantees   2
   The Dawning of Doubts about FSLIC   7
    Economic Insolvency   8
    Solvency vs. Liquidity of FSLIC   10
   Aggregate Measures of Thrift Profitability   10
   Zombies are Ponzis   17
   The Policy Impasse: The Siren Song of
    Procrastination   18

**2 Risk, S&L Capital, and the Framework of FSLIC
Regulation**   23
   Different Professions' Definitions of an Individual
    Firm's Capital   23
   What is Capital for FSLIC?   24
   The Capital Adequacy Question   29
   Background Summary of Industry Problems and
    Federal Government Responses   32
   Incentive Conflicts between FSLIC and Insolvent
    Clients: The Wisdom of Throwing the Long
    Ball   33
   Political Roots and Economic Effects of Capital
    Forbearance Extended in the Mid-980s   51
   The Efficiency of Managerial Tradeoffs between
    Risk and Reward   57
    *Distinguishing Go-for-Broke Financial Plays from
     Managerial Corruption and Negligence* 58
    *Managerial Efficiency in FSLIC Liquidation and
     Nationalization Activities*   60

Summary and Transition   61

**3 Identifying and Understanding FSLIC's Critical
Mistakes**   63
Innocent versus Guilty Mistakes   63
Layering of Incentive Incompatibilities   66
Turning a Blind Eye to the Unbooked Interest-
    Induced Decapitalization of Thrift
    Institutions   70
    Interest-Rate Risk: Roots and Consequences   72
    The Size of the Pre-Deregulation Interest-Induced
        Decapitalization of FSLIC-Insured
        Institutions   75
Two Ways to Reserve for the Asset-Quality
    Problems Developing after 1982   76
    A Procedure for Calculating FSLIC's Loss
        Exposure in Insolvent Institutions Only   78
    A More General Loss-Calculation Procedure   79
    Rates of Deposit Interest Paid by GAAP-Insolvent
        Thrifts   85
The Impact of Expanded Thrift Powers: Refuting a
    Bad Rap   87
Summary and Transition   92

**4 Socially Perverse Incentives Confronting Thrift
Regulators**   95
The Looting of FSLIC   95
Changes in FSLIC's Regulatory Strategy   98
A Model of Changes in Regulatory Incentives   101
Role of Agency Costs   105
Agency Costs and Congressionally Mandated
    Ceilings on Top Officials' Explicit Salaries   106
Where We Are Now   109
Appendix: An Algebraic Summary of the Argument   115
Looking at FSLIC as a Government-Controlled
    Corporation   115
Valuing a Deposit-Insurance Enterprise   116
Implications for Optimally Managing FSLIC
    Cash Flows   119

5 **Evidence of Regulatory Gambling: The Meltdowns of Two Deposit-Insurance Funds**   121
    Where to Look for Empirical Evidence for or against
        the Incentive-Breakdown Hypothesis   121
    The Six Stages of a Deposit-Insurance Meltdown   123
    Evidence of Regulatory Gambling in Ohio and
        Maryland   129
        The Ohio Case   129
        The Maryland Case   136
    Regulatory Coverup and Gambling in Radioactive
        Waste   140
    Summary and Transition   141

6 **Guidelines for Salient Reform**   145
    The Immediate Problem   147
        Four Distracting Cosmetic Issues   148
        Who Should Pay?   150
        De Facto Nationalization   152
        Controlling Potential Inefficiencies in the
            Reprivatization Process   154
        The February 1989 Bush Initiative for Corralling
            Current Zombies   156
        Neglected Portions of FSLIC's Unpaid Bills   157
    The Long-Run Problem   158
        Improving the Incentive System for Deposit
            Insurers   159
        Improving the Incentive System for Politicians   161
        Improving the Incentive System for Insured
            Institutions   162
        Emphasizing Market Discipline: Automatic
            Reassessment of Deposit-Insurance
            Premiums   164
        Emphasizing Regulatory Discipline: Less-
            Discretionary Capital Adequacy
            Requirements   167
    Summary   176
        The Stubbornness of Subsidies   177
        Making Congress Accountable for Backdoor
            Spending   178

Tables

1.1   Official Estimates of FSLIC Reserves, 1960–87   9
1.2   Average Explicit Earnings Spread on New
       Mortgage Lending at FSLIC-Insured
       Institutions, 1965–87   12
1.3   Alternating Profitability Ratios Observed for
       Federally Insured Savings Institutions,
       1960–87   14
2.1   Number of GAAP Insolvencies and Insolvency
       Resolutions at FSLIC-Insured Institutions,
       1975–88   26
2.2   Tally of Administrative Initiatives by FSLIC to
       Discipline Individual S&L Managements,
       1980–86   27
2.3   Major Federal Laws Affecting the Savings
       Institution Business, 1932–87   34
2.4   Major Regulatory Changes Affecting Savings
       Institutions, 1981–87   38
2.5   Comparison of Mean Market Capitalization
       with Mean Asset Size for 32 Selected Thrift
       Institutions, 1985–86, by Quarter   49
2.6   Top Beneficiaries from S&L PAC Donations   53
2.7   Number and Asset Size of FSLIC-Insured
       Institutions with Year-End Examination
       Ratings of 4 or 5, 1980–84   55
2.8   Accuracy of FSLIC's 1980–84 Year-End
       Examination Ratings as Proxy Forecasts for
       the Number of Insolvency Resolutions and
       GAAP-Insolvent Thrifts Observed in the
       Succeeding Year   56
3.1   Estimates of the Ratio of Market-Value Net
       Worth to Total Assets at FSLIC-Insured
       Thrifts, 1971–84   75
3.2   Number of Thrifts that Veribanc, Inc.
       Determined to Be Suffering from Various
       Unfavorable Conditions, 1984–88, by
       Quarter   80
3.3   Income, Capital and Real Estate Owned
       Recorded for Insolvent Thrifts, 1987–88, by
       Quarter   82

3.4 Ballpark Estimate of the Accumulating
     Imbedded Loss to FSLIC that is Embodied
     in the Operations of GAAP-Like Insolvent
     and Tangible-Insolvent Firms, 1987–88, by
     Quarter   84
3.5 Calculation of FSLIC's Average Insolvency-
     Resolution Cost Rate in Liquidations and
     Assisted Resolutions, 1934–88   86
3.6 Alternative Estimate of FSLIC Losses
     Imbedded in the Operations of GAAP-
     Insolvent Thrifts, 1982–88   87
3.7 Evidence on Offering Interest Rates on Thrift
     CDs, March 1987 to September 1988   88
3.8 Differences in the Ratios of Selected Balance-
     Sheet Positions to Total Assets at GAAP-
     Solvent and GAAP-Insolvent Thrifts Insured
     by FSLIC, 1982 to mid-1988   90
3.9 Comparison of Differences in the Capital
     Positions of GAAP-Solvent and GAAP-
     Insolvent Thrifts with Maximal
     Hypothetical Losses on Differences in
     Nontraditional Loans and Investments,
     1982–88   92
4.1 Estimate of Size of FSLIC's Examination and
     Supervisory Resources in Selected Years,
     1936–86   101
A.4.1 Uncontrolled, Partially Controlled, and
     Control Variables Affecting the Value of
     FSLIC's Pseudo-Stock Price   120
5.1 Reported Size of Home State Savings, at
     Selected Dates during 1979–85   132
5.1A Ticking Time Bomb Memo Filed on Home
     State Savings by ODSL Examiner in Early
     1983   133
5.2 Comparison of Weighted Average Explicit
     Deposit Interest Rates at Home State
     Savings and FSLIC-Insured Savings
     Institutions at Selected Dates, 1978–85   134
5.3 Chronology of Regulatory Gambling during
     ODGF's Loss-Generation Stage   135

5.4   Chronology of Regulatory Gambling prior to
the Maryland Savings-Share Insurance
Corporation Crisis   137
About the Author   181

Insolvency in the thrift industry is now a major national embarrassment. With the taxpayer debt estimated at $100 billion or more and rising daily, the nation can ill afford further delay in providing a lasting solution. Edward Kane's timely book makes an important contribution to the debate about what that solution should be.

Banking issues are not central to the work of the Institute. However, identifying national problems,and bringing the best information and scholarship to bear on developing solutions, has been our explicit mission since we were established by Congress. The crisis facing the nation when the Institute was established in 1968 was the rioting in our center cities. The insurance problem in the thrift industry may be less dramatic, but it is probably no less serious.

Through the efforts of Rudolph Penner, Senior Fellow at the Institute, we have been fortunate to persuade Ed Kane, a serious scholar who predicted the emerging crisis several years ago, to write a book giving a full appreciation of the nature of the problem. Ed Kane's views are his own, but his credentials for the task are plain for all to see, and his views merit serious consideration.

The message is a sobering one. In his view, the root cause of the crisis is neither a few specific regulatory mistakes nor corruption by a group of unscrupulous people in the Savings and Loan industry. The problem is the result of structural flaws in the system. Because of these flaws, the industry and its regulators, which include the United States Congress, are faced with virtually irresistible incentives to ignore signals of pending insolvency, and to postpone the inevitable day of reckoning until "someone else" takes over and becomes responsible.

At stake here is more than the fate of the S&L industry and the size of the bill that will eventually face the U.S. taxpayer. So much in our society—indeed in any society—depends on a whole set of presuppositions about the fundamental viability of its institutions. Major threats to any one institution weaken all institutions. Ed Kane's diagnosis of the problems in the thrift industry provides an object lesson on the need to be alert to the fundamental incentives embedded in *all* our institutions—and to examine them periodically rather than waiting for a costly and ultimately destructive crisis to erupt.

William Gorham
President

Chapter One

ZOMBIE THRIFTS AND FSLIC:
A FEDERAL PONZI SCHEME?

Red ink is a symbol for stubborn losses and for stubborn stains. During the last 25 years, the savings and loan associations (S&Ls) and savings banks that constitute the U.S. thrift industry have spilled a flood of red ink. This red ink spread effectively over the balance sheet of the industry's chief deposit insurer: the Federal Savings and Loan Insurance Corporation or FSLIC (pronounced "Fizz-lick"). Rather than immediately facing up to this problem, for a long while federal regulators and federal politicians let accounting gimmicks render the damage invisible to ordinary citizens. Hiding the stains and deferring the cleanup for so long greatly compounded the aggregate mess.

The book's central message is that congressional procedures for budgeting and for overseeing the operations of the deposit-insurance bureaucracy made the regulatory strategy of coverup and deferral practically irresistible. To see this, it is helpful to contemplate a perspective-setting parable. The parable concerns a few members of Congress who, after a hard day of making laws, set out to relax by going out for dinner. As political celebrities patronizing a D.C. restaurant, they soon find themselves seated at a prominent table. The prominence of their table tempts them to order the most expensive food and wine on the menu, on the gamble that a lobbyist at some other table will notice them and pick up their check. They confidently expect the restaurant manager to fill even the most lavish orders. He does not worry about how much cash or what credit cards individual members of the dinner party may have brought with them. He is confident that one way or another *someone* will pay these customers' bill in full. With the same confidence, the members of the dinner party end up staying at their table for an uncomfortably long time and even order an unwanted round or two of after-dinner drinks to give potential volunteers more time to grab their growing check.

A parallel exists between this growing dinner bill and the unallocated deposit-institution losses that accumulated in state-sponsored deposit-insurance funds in recent years and are still accumulating in FSLIC and in the Federal Deposit Insurance Corporation (FDIC). Congress has repeatedly let the serious financial shortages at FSLIC and many individual deposit institutions ride. Rather than submitting the bill that FSLIC has run up to taxpayers for immediate payment, Congress has been hoping for insured institutions' imbedded losses to be cured by various lucky movements in real estate, farm, energy, and bond prices and in the economies of less developed countries. The Federal Home Loan Bank Board (FHLBB), the General Accounting Office (GAO), and private experts all agree that since 1983 FSLIC and the FDIC have lost billions of dollars while waiting for their luck in high-risk financial enterprises to change.

In dealing with the thrift industry, politicians are of two minds. They seek alternately to assist and to constrain it. This split personality exists because politicians have many forms of ongoing dealings with industry managers and trade associations, and also because congressional committees and the executive arm of the federal government are split into enterprises whose primary missions are essentially single-purpose ones (tax collection, industry regulation, housing promotion, mortgage finance). It is nobody's business to look at all facets of the industry together.

THE BLACK MAGIC OF FEDERAL GUARANTEES

The U.S. thrift industry acquired its name because its primary members feature the word "savings" in their official titles. However, this characterization is incomplete. The words *thrift* and *savings* emphasize only the fund-raising half of these financial firms' traditional twin specializations. No firm can make a living merely by issuing and servicing financial instruments in which households can reasonably plan to store their savings. To generate revenues, thrift managers must also put the funds they raise to work on their firms' behalf. This asset-management half of the thrift game involves reinvesting the funds savers entrust to these institutions into higher yielding assets. Traditionally and even during the freewheeling 1980s, the largest proportion of these earning assets has consisted of residential mortgage loans.

The flowchart of business activity I just sketched—from storing savings to asset management—can be instructively reversed. Thrifts may equally well be viewed as transforming the earning assets they want to purchase into savings vehicles that households find attractive to hold. Most household savers prefer to put their funds into instruments that are safer and more liquid than mortgage loans. Thrift institution deposit accounts have been perceived to be particularly safe because, for amounts up to $100,000, repayment is fully guaranteed by FSLIC.

These fund-raising and asset-management activities of thrift managers simultaneously provide service benefits to a thrift's customers and impose costs on the thrift. It is a central theme of this book that service benefits and costs are just as important to the financial picture of a thrift as are the explicit earnings and interest flows that appear on the traditional income statement. In particular, for a thrift to stay in business in the long run, it must be able to make enough on the spread between what its assets return and the interest it pays out to its depositors to cover these costs and still have enough profits left over to survive.

This can be made clearer by viewing thrifts as buying or "renting" funds at one price and trying to lend them out again at an even higher fee. Interest is the compensation paid per period for the use of funds. Calling interest paid in cash explicit interest assigns the name "implicit interest" to the value of services and other noncash premiums that a lender may receive. Explicit interest is sometimes thought of as *de jure* interest (interest according to law). This view leads one to describe the sum of explicit and implicit interest as *de facto* interest (interest that reflects the complete facts of the situation).

To make a profit, the interest a thrift earns on its loans and investments must exceed the total or *de facto* interest a thrift pays its depositors and nondeposit creditors. In recent years, macroeconomic, technological, and regulatory developments have put this interest spread—and therefore the many institutions that extract their living from it—under considerable pressure.

As the pressure intensified, more and more deposit institutions began to experience financial problems. In the last few years, officials have begun to worry openly about the large number of severely weakened thrift institutions in operation. Since about 1984, between 600 and 800 thrift institutions have been hopelessly insolvent. This amounts to about 25 percent of the number of firms in the thrift industry. The net value of these crippled firms' assets has sunk so far under water that their managers' only hope of becoming profitable again has been to expand their firms' funding base and to invest the new funds they raise in a speculative manner. The idea is to "grow out of their problems" by undertaking longshot new lending and funding activities that essentially renew and expand (or "double up") the lost bets of the past. If their bets pay off, these firms regain solvency. If they lose, their problems belong to FSLIC.

An apt name for these insolvent hellbent-for-leather thrifts is institutional zombies. The economic life they enjoy is an unnatural life-in-death existence in that, if they had not been insured, the firms' creditors would have taken control from stockholders once it became clear that their enterprises' net worth was exhausted. In effect, a zombie has transcended its natural death from accumulated losses by the black magic of federal guarantees.

To appreciate the magic, we must understand that deposit insurance is not strictly insurance at all. This is because FSLIC guarantees are not written against a specified set of risks whose actuarial potential to destroy the institution's financial viability can be calculated in advance. Because the guarantee contract does not limit the set of unfavorable events to which the guarantor's credit is exposed, and because the degree of effective risk can be increased by the guaranteed party, deposit insurance represents an unconditional third-party guarantee of a firm's capacity to repay a particular class of its debts.

Credible guarantees enhance the credit of a borrower. They permit an institution to finance its operations at a lower cost or with less stockholder-contributed capital than it would otherwise. Unlike a healthy thrift, the value of zombie firms to their stockholders is not rooted in a reasonable expectation that future profits will ordinarily be generated by the assets these firms hold. To the contrary, the only value of these firms lies in their longshot chances to make a big killing. A zombie's ability to issue and service debt, therefore, is entirely dependent on its capacity to transfer most of its losses effectively to FSLIC. Because uninsured creditors will obviously resist lending to a zombie firm, it is clear that substantial subsidies are implicit in the relatively low-cost guarantees that holders of a zombie's deposits receive through the federal deposit-insurance system. As long as depositors trust in these subsidized guarantees, they need not fret about the tenuous profitability of the uses to which the zombie's managers put their funds.

Because federal credit enhancements cut the link between the riskiness of the assets an institution holds and its capacity to raise funding for these assets, zombie firms are attracted to socially inappropriate forms of risk taking. The inappropriateness lies in the fact that on average the risks they take are bad deals for FSLIC and federal tax-payers, who turn out to be the zombies' true victims. Federal regulatory officials and congressional oversight committees were warned long ago about the high cost of enhancing the credit of zombie firms and about the dangers inherent in letting their managers expand these firms with federally insured debt. However, rather than taking the proverbial ounce of prevention by corralling zombie institutions, authorities at the FHLBB and at its GAO auditor have systematically used accounting discretion to understate the depth and breadth of industry problems. Hiding individual firms' economic insolvencies from the public temporarily makes federal officials appear to be more successful regulators than they truly are. However, it also permits zombie firms to continue to issue more deposits and to collateralize other forms of debt. Delaying the resolution of their insolvency encourages them to take deep risks with the funds they do attract.

These policies of coverup and delay amount to a possibly unconscious form of longshot regulatory gambling that closely parallels the gambling in which the zombie firms themselves are engaged. Deferring action allows authorities to shift formal recognition of the industry's ongoing problems to someone else's watch. For taxpayers and the deposit-insurance funds, this procrastination is shortsighted because it tends to increase the size and range of the deposit industry's problems in the long run. Permitting zombie firms to continue operations creates new generations of zombies by draining away some of the profitability of the healthy segment of the depository industry. Zombie firms depress industry profit margins by bidding down interest rates on loans and bidding up interest rates on deposits to unsustainable levels. Moreover, the losses zombie firms experience on average deepen the aggregate insolvency facing FSLIC. The insurer's eventual need to finance these losses further hurts industry profitability by increasing the value of the future deposit-insurance premiums that solvent institutions must expect to pay.

Conventional wisdom holds that a firm becomes financially weak because of inept management, dishonest behavior, or unfavorable conditions in the markets the firm serves. The weaknesses we now observe in the thrift industry and in FSLIC parody this view. Ironically, a root cause of much of the thrift-industry crisis is *clever* management. Of course, this cleverness is in the end undone by collisions with the three conventional sources of weakness just described. But these conventional factors frequently serve a secondary role. In most cases, the aggressive, freewheeling growth and investment policies adopted by zombie thrifts are managerially sound ones, in the sense that when they are first undertaken they increase the market value of the firms adopting them.

Even if the projects financed eventually go bad, unless fraud is involved, the investments made are not bad at their outset. This is because a zombie firm reaps an advantage from the asymmetry of its stake in the outcome of high-risk opportunities. It gets to keep a major share of any profits; FSLIC gets the losses. The degree of asymmetry decreases with the strength of the guaranteed institution's capital position and increases with the riskiness of its operations. To clarify this, it is instructive to think of a risky loan or investment as equivalent to a bet placed in a casino game of chance that would offer the same odds of success as whatever project the zombie thrift is actually financing. In effect, FSLIC's unconditional willingness to repay the zombie's depositors allows its managers to open up a line of credit in any financial casino they can enter. This line of credit permits the zombie to book high-stakes bets even though it has no funds of its own to risk. The guarantees that FSLIC offers to the zombie's insured depositors leaves them relatively unconcerned about how the zombie's bets actually turn out. Deposit insurance shifts the deep downside of the zombie's risky bets to FSLIC and to the unknown federal taxpayers that ultimately back up FSLIC. At the same time, owners and managers of the zombie firm are entitled to receive interim payments and to keep the lion's share of the upside returns on the longshot bets they manage to place.

The subsidy to risk taking that a zombie thrift enjoys in booking risky projects may be defined as the capitalized value of the reduction in the zombie's cost of funding its portfolio that deposit insurance allows. In the absence of FSLIC guarantees, a zombie would have to contract to pass through to its depositors whatever risk premium it may expect to earn on its portfolio of loans and investments. In the presence of FSLIC insurance, the zombie keeps this risk premium and pays out instead whatever costs are generated by the explicit fees, administrative burdens, and activity restrictions that the deposit insurer imposes on its clients.

Managerial cleverness lies in taking advantage of subsidies to risk taking implicit in the way deposit-insurance has been priced and administered by Congress and FSLIC. Through 1984, the annual explicit premium for FSLIC insurance was $\frac{1}{12}$ of 1 percent of an institution's deposits. Since 1985, an additional surcharge of $\frac{1}{8}$ of 1 percent has been added, bringing the overall charge to $\frac{5}{24}$ of 1 percent. Because this explicit premium does not increase with the riskiness of an insured firm's operations, FSLIC insurance can simultaneously be unreasonably expensive for a conservatively run firm and unreasonably cheap for an aggressively run enterprise that has little of its own capital at risk.

In effect, federal authorities offer incentive payments to under-capitalized thrifts and to any thrift whose managers are willing and able to skew their investments toward aggressive, high-risk deals. In turn, the pricing and risk-management decisions that feed these incentives were made by Congress and FSLIC in ways that may be interpreted as having served officials' short-term personal or bureaucratic interests all too well. Managers' and officials' cleverness took advantage of naive and underinformed taxpayers, whose too-trusting passiveness marks them as the truly inept and unaware players in zombie enterprises.

Over time, subsidies tend to weaken the moral and competitive "muscles" of those that receive them. Hence, it should be no surprise to learn that corruption and unfavorable economic conditions followed in the wake of these policies and greatly aggravated the losses that FSLIC and its weakest clients eventually experienced.

In what might or might not turn out to be a pivotal case, a federal judge, Jack B. Weinstein, held U.S. regulators and lawmakers to blame (as this book does) for the high-risk loans that ruined Flushing Federal S&L in New York. As reported in the Law Section of the February 27, 1989 *Wall Street Journal*, his opinion cited testimony that FHLBB officials had encouraged Flushing's directors to be less conservative in their lending because the association was running at a loss. After noting that this does not condone criminal and incompetent activity, he wrote: "Congress and the Home Loan Bank Board are directly responsible for what happened here. The government, in removing adequate controls over this bank, led to the activities now complained of." He went on to note that Flushing's losses were a "microcosm" of the billions of dollars of losses that are "a result of the failure of the federal government to do what it should have done in supervising and controlling" thrift institutions.

THE DAWNING OF DOUBTS ABOUT FSLIC

A well-managed private guarantor acknowledges foreseeable losses by setting up a reserve account large enough to cover them when they come due. FSLIC's record contrasts sharply with this standard. Since the end of 1983, official accounting measures of FSLIC's gross reserves have shrunk from roughly $6.5 billion to less than $2 billion dollars. During the same interval, responsible estimates of the losses imbedded in the guarantees FSLIC has written have surged into the range of $100 to $150 billion. This means that, once analysts reserve conscientiously for FSLIC's imbedded or *de facto* losses, its net reserves become highly negative. President Bush has explicitly recognized that a taxpayer-funded bailout of FSLIC is politically inescapable and that the bill the taxpayer faces grows larger the longer federal politicians wait to present it.

To assess this bill, it is necessary to look at FSLIC's finances in a disciplined way. A balance sheet is an accounting scheme for sorting out the corporate assets and liabilities that underlie a firm's future flows of net income. Each asset and liability item represents the capitalized value of a particular set of projected future cash flows. The aggregate value of the net assets reported on any entity's balance sheet is called its net worth.

An explicit balance sheet can be drawn up to itemize FSLIC's assets and liabilities in different ways. Each of these different ways sorts through FSLIC finances according to itemization and valuation schemes embodied in a recognized system of accounting. Today, no matter what system of accounting we use, once we allow for the obligations generated by losses imbedded in its client base, FSLIC's explicit balance sheet has a large hole in it. FSLIC's explicit corporate assets simply do not have the capacity to service its explicit liabilities as these accrue and come due. Table 1-1 reproduces the relatively conservative assessment issued jointly by the FHLBB and GAO of how FSLIC's reserve position evolved from 1960 to 1987. This assessment tends to overstate the market value of FSLIC reserves at each date and to make the agency's slide into a negative reserve position misleadingly appear to be a recent and sudden phenomenon.

Economic Insolvency

An institution is commonly said to be insolvent when it has lost the capacity to discharge its liabilities. However, this definition does not allow us to understand the S&L mess because it is incomplete in two ways. First, it fails to specify whether the failure to discharge liabilities reflects merely a temporary lack of liquidity or an insufficiency in the underlying value of the firm's net assets. Second, the definition fails to distinguish the possibility that a firm may be able to discharge its liabilities only because of credit enhancements furnished at a subsidy by an outside guarantor.

Table 1-1 OFFICIAL ESTIMATES OF FSLIC RESERVES, 1960–87

Year End	Total Reserves ($ million)	Percentage of Insured Liability[a]
1960	381	0.62%
1965	1,537	1.35
1970	2,903	2.05
1971	2,987	1.77
1972	3,142	1.56
1973	3,454	1.56
1974	3,791	1.60
1975	4,120	1.48
1976	4,480	1.37
1977	4,873	1.29
1978	5,328	1.26
1979	5,848	1.27
1980	6,462	1.28
1981	6,156	1.18
1982	6,307	1.13
1983	6,425	0.96
1984	5,600	0.71
1985	4,600	0.54
1986	−6,300	−0.71
1987	−13,700[b]	−1.47

Source: 1960–79: United States League of Savings Institutions, *1988 Savings Institutions Sourcebook*, p. 63; 1980–87: Federal Home Loan Bank Board, *1987 Annual Report*.
a. Reserves as a percentage of the total accounts of insured depositors at all insured institutions.
b. Estimated.

By an economically insolvent thrift, I mean a condition in which the market value of the firm's enterprise-contributed net worth is negative. The term "enterprise-contributed" is introduced to strip out the value of FSLIC guarantees. The term "economic" is employed to convey the idea that a complete analysis of a corporation's financial condition must look at implicit (or invisible) assets and liabilities as well as explicit ones. Implicit claims and obligations may be defined as sources of future cash flows that are treated as "off-balance-sheet items" by the particular accounting system under which a given balance sheet is developed. Traditional accounting schemes look only at an entity's explicit assets and liabilities, and assess specific forms of explicit *accounting* solvency only.

Solvency vs. Liquidity of FSLIC

Joint congressional resolutions passed in 1982 and 1987 and the promises made by President Bush on February 6, 1989 may be interpreted as assigning FSLIC an implicit asset that amounts to a nearly unlimited call on taxpayer resources. Nevertheless, until legislation necessary to define this asset explicitly is passed, FSLIC can be termed explicitly insolvent.

Explicit insolvency does not mean that FSLIC can no longer cover its maturing obligations. However, public confidence in the nation's weakest S&Ls has been shaken. If authorities do anything that is construed to disadvantage insured depositors, zombie firms would begin to experience deposit runs that they could not cover. If higher authorities did not step in promptly to arrest the process in some way (for example, by lending aggressively through the Federal Reserve's discount window), an industrywide disaster could result.

As in any disaster, people would be hurt and a considerable amount of property would be lost. Carnage and property damage can be lessened when community leaders undertake watchful action in advance of the ruinous central event and prompt remedial action in its aftermath. In the slow decline of FSLIC, authorities have been insufficiently watchful and inordinately loath to adopt proper remedies. It is for this reason that any FSLIC disaster would deserve the label "made in Washington." It would more closely resemble a massacre of civilians by a misdirected cadre of government forces than it would resemble a natural disaster unleashed by inherently uncontrollable forces such as windstorms, earthquakes, or floods.

AGGREGATE MEASURES OF THRIFT PROFITABILITY

For thrift institutions insured by FSLIC, Table 1-2 calculates the earnings spread observed in 1960–87 between the average interest rate on an important type of mortgage loan and the explicit interest cost of savings deposits. As already explained, this is not the same as the average economic profit earned by these institutions. To calculate the average *economic profits* earned on mortgages in any year by FSLIC-insured thrifts, two additional elements must be introduced.

First, we must incorporate a measure of the costs of providing convenience and other services to borrowers and depositors. As a rough approximation, these costs may be proxied by FSLIC-insured institutions' average ratio of operating expense to assets, a factor that has trended sharply upward over time. The last column of Table 1-2 calculates a spread that deducts these costs. This adjusted spread shows that new mortgage lending has been profitable in every year covered, but that the average net earnings spread on new mortgages peaked in 1981 and has been decreasing on average ever since. This narrowing spread reflects three forces: reduced compensation for the option to prepay that mortgage borrowers receive (this option's value decreases as contract interest rates decline), and the unfavorable impact on industry profit margins of zombie thrifts and of expanded competition from securities-industry involvement in mortgage banking activities. Mortgage banking may be defined as financing mortgages by pooling and reselling principal and interest payments in government-assisted securities markets.

Second, it is necessary to allow for changes in the market value of the portfolio of mortgages held. To do this, we must construct a measure of booked and unbooked capital gains or losses on outstanding mortgages that are caused by borrower defaults and changes in interest rates. Allowing for these factors introduces an element of profit that rises when mortgage interest rates fall and falls when mortgage interest rates rise.

Table 1-3 reports the average annual return on total thrift assets (mortgage and nonmortgage investments) and three measures of the net profitability of thrift operations since 1960. Separate figures are reported for FSLIC-insured firms and for thrifts that are insured by the Federal Deposit Insurance Corporation (FDIC). FDIC-insured thrifts consist of state-chartered savings banks and federally chartered institutions that switched their insurance from FSLIC before a congressional moratorium on such switches was imposed in 1987. The number of these firms grew from 325 in 1960 to 485 in 1987.

The profitability measures only recognize *booked* (or realized) losses or gains on mortgage defaults or recoveries and on mortgage sales. They take no account of accrued but unbooked capital gains and losses. Decisions as to whether or not to realize an unbooked gain or loss gives a firm's managers a discretionary opportunity to window-dress their reported condition. Omitting the accrual element distorts the timing of profit flows. It does this not only by failing to book capital losses and gains as they accrue, but by transforming these losses and gains into below-market or above-market rates of

Table 1-2 AVERAGE EXPLICIT EARNINGS SPREAD ON NEW MORTGAGE LENDING AT FSLIC-INSURED
INSTITUTIONS, 1965–87 (percent per annum)

Year	Effective Interest Rate on Conventional Loans on New Homes (1)	Explicit Interest Cost of Savings Deposits in FSLIC-Insured Savings Institutions (2)	Average Explicit Earnings Spread on New-Home Mortgage Lending (3) = (1) − (2)	Operating-Expense Ratio for FSLIC-Insured Institutions (4)	Average Net Earnings Spread on New-Home Mortgages (5) = (3) − (4)
1965	5.81	4.25	1.56	1.06	0.50
1970	8.45	5.14	3.31	1.11	2.20
1971	7.74	5.30	2.44	1.06	1.35
1972	7.60	5.37	2.23	1.05	1.18
1973	7.96[a]	5.51	2.45	1.03	1.42
1974	8.92	5.96	2.96	1.19	1.77
1975	9.00	6.21	2.79	1.20	1.59
1976	9.00	6.31	2.69	1.20	1.49
1977	9.02	6.39	2.63	1.18	1.45

1978	9.56	6.56	3.00	1.20	1.80
1979	10.78	7.29	3.49	1.25	2.24
1980	12.66	8.78	3.88	1.28	2.60
1981	14.70	10.71	3.99	1.38	2.61
1982	15.14	11.19	3.95	1.44	2.51
1983	12.57	9.71	2.86	1.50	1.36
1984	12.38	9.93	2.45	1.57	0.88
1985	11.55	9.03	2.52	1.83	0.69
1986	10.17	7.84	2.33	1.97	0.36
1987	9.31	6.92[b]	2.39	1.94	0.45

Source: Columns 1 and 2 are taken from United States League of Savings Association, *1988 Savings Institutions Sourcebook*, pp. 31 and 25. Savings Deposits are defined to include all types of savings; by 1987 this includes passbook, NOW and Super NOW, Money Market, and fixed-maturity accounts. Column 4 is calculated as the ratio of operating expense to total assets, using figures given on pp. 48–50 of the *1988 Savings Institution Sourcebook*.

a. New series.
b. Preliminary.

Table 1-3 ALTERNATIVE PROFITABILITY RATIOS OBSERVED FOR FEDERALLY INSURED SAVINGS INSTITUTIONS, 1960–87

	FSLIC-Insured Savings Institutions				FDIC-Insured Savings Banks			
Year	Gross Return on Assets[a]	Profit Margin[b]	Return on Equity[c]	Return on Average Assets[d]	Gross Return on Assets[a]	Profit Margin[b]	Return on Equity[c]	Return on Average Assets[d]
1960	5.55%	15.55%	12.35%	0.86%	4.25%	11.50%	5.76%	0.49%
1965	5.72	11.63	9.83	0.67	4.93	9.33	5.83	0.46
1970	6.60	8.56	8.02	0.57	5.87	4.31	3.37	0.25
1971	6.93	10.24	10.51	0.71	6.15	7.59	6.56	0.47
1972	7.02	11.01	12.14	0.77	6.38	9.05	8.41	0.58
1973	7.34	10.31	12.15	0.76	6.68	7.88	7.64	0.53
1974	7.63	7.03	8.63	0.54	6.87	4.89	4.85	0.33
1975	7.73	6.06	7.82	0.47	7.06	5.08	5.30	0.36
1976	8.01	7.87	11.10	0.63	7.29	6.09	6.81	0.44
1977	8.23	9.32	13.94	0.77	7.43	7.23	8.39	0.54
1978	8.50	9.57	14.84	0.82	7.75	7.58	9.09	0.59

1979	9.08	7.37	12.06	0.67	8.24	5.42	6.79	0.45
1980	9.60	1.38	2.44	0.13	8.67	-1.58	-2.56	-0.17
1981	10.48	-6.96	-15.44	-0.73	9.47	-9.91	-16.21	-0.94
1982	11.27	-5.64	-16.13	-0.65	9.72	-8.21	-15.77	-0.80
1983	11.20	2.34	6.77	0.27	9.76	-1.07	-2.16	-0.10
1984	11.66	1.05	3.15	0.13	10.35	0.68	1.56	0.07
1985	11.49	3.27	9.14	0.39	10.61	7.11	14.49	0.75
1986	10.68	0.08	0.20	0.01	10.15	10.55	16.21	1.07
1987e	9.44	-6.00	-13.10	-0.56	n.a.	n.a.	n.a.	n.a.

Source: United States League of Savings Associations, 1988 Savings Institution Sourcebook, p. 53.
Note: Beginning in 1982, average assets exclude certain contra-asset balances that had been reported as liabilities.
a. Total income divided by average assets (net of loans in process or contra-assets).
b. Net after-tax income divided by total income.
c. Net after-tax income divided by average net worth.
d. Net after-tax income divided by average assets (net of loans in process or contra-assets).
e. Preliminary.
n.a. = not available.

future earnings. In particular, most of the negative profits FSLIC institutions report for 1987 reflect losses carried over in unbooked form from the past.

Still, even these relatively imperfect figures support two important inferences. First, 1981 and 1982 were tough years for all thrifts. Second, both in the preceding year and in the following year, FDIC-insured thrifts appear to have booked more capital losses than FSLIC thrifts. This suggests that accounting figures for FDIC-insured thrifts may be less distorted than those for FSLIC firms. Second, the higher gross returns on assets reported each year for FSLIC thrifts suggest that, throughout the time period examined, these firms have systematically held a higher risk, higher return set of assets than FDIC-insured thrifts have.

Industrywide profitability problems seldom develop suddenly and unexpectedly. Typically, subtle and unsubtle economic forces eat away at industry profit margins slowly over many months, much as water erodes the surface of a stone over which it flows.

For pre-1980 thrift firms, the heart of the industry's profit margin was the earnings spread between: the yield earned on a portfolio consisting of mortgage loans and a narrow set of other permissible investments, on the one hand, and the explicit and implicit interest cost of its deposit and nondeposit debt, on the other.

Institutions are said to be short-funded when they use short-term debt to fund holdings of long-term assets that have contractually fixed interest rates. Such institutions expose their earnings spread to risks from interest rate increases and interest volatility. These risks exist because upward surges in interest rates require a downward movement in the market value of these institution's portfolios of older low-rate loans. When interest rates rise, the implied capital loss can easily overwhelm a thrift's explicit interest earnings from outstanding mortgage loans. Another way of saying this is to observe that, because its liabilities roll over faster than its assets, the funding cost of a short-funded institution is going to prove more sensitive to interest rate changes than the yields it earns on the asset side of its portfolio. For this reason, *unanticipated* increases in interest rates tend to narrow thrift spreads and may even turn them negative. Interest-volatility risk adds to this risk, in the sense that the wider the range over which interest rates swing in a typical boom, the more easily a thrift may become economically insolvent and the larger the number of mortgagors who prepay their mortgage loans when interest rates decline.

Elected officials have long shown a propensity to subsidize home-ownership through government-sponsored schemes to support housing finance. This propensity helps to explain why, until the mid-1980s, federal authorities chose implicitly to underwrite thrifts' interest rate risk. They did this by keeping most of the losses induced by interest rate increases from having to be acknowledged and passed through either to stockholders or to depositors. Subsidized federal deposit insurance effectively stripped the worst of this risk away from the industry and loaded it instead onto FSLIC. FSLIC guarantees helped to increase both the size and riskiness of the thrift industry. The existence of these guarantees permitted even economically insolvent deposit institutions not only to stay in business, but even to undertake a series of go-for-broke loans and investments that they were allowed to finance with funds raised from customers at roughly the low funding cost applicable to U.S. Treasury debt.

ZOMBIES ARE PONZIS

It is instructive to compare a zombie thrift institution with an illegal Ponzi or pyramid scheme. The name Ponzi commemorates the brainstorm and abbreviated financial career of an infamous conman, Charles Ponzi, who operated in Boston around 1920. In a Ponzi scheme, a fund-raising enterprise operates with little or none of the earning assets that a sound enterprise requires to generate a projected stream of cash flows with which to service lenders and investors. Instead, the enterprise relies on expanding its liabilities faster than its interest and dividend payments expand. The enterprise pays interest or dividends each period to its old clients—not from earnings but from funds that are provided by new lenders and investors. As long as new funds can be attracted into the scheme fast enough, the enterprise's managers can meet corporate obligations as they come due and pay themselves handsomely at the same time. This can only be done, of course by making seductive promises of high returns and making the scheme's subscribers believe these promises to be reasonable.

The flaw in any Ponzi scheme is that in the end the promises being made have no collective chance of being kept. Until a day of reckoning dawns, however, the sponsors' false promises are mistaken for truth and participants in the scheme appear to prosper. The apparent prosperity of the enterprise tends to disarm critics of the scheme by giving them the appearance of individuals who lack imagination or vision.

A Ponzi scheme is a classic case of value created in the marketplace by asymmetries in the distribution of information. The scheme's sponsors know that they are running a con game, but subscribers do not. Keeping subscribers and potential critics from learning or guessing this hidden information becomes increasingly difficult the longer the scheme goes on. Once economically unsound elements in the scheme begin to surface—as inevitably they must—public confidence and the value of subscribers' claims to future cash flows can collapse rapidly.

To an important extent, zombie thrifts and FSLIC itself became interconnected Ponzi schemes. Confidence in zombies' and FSLIC's continuing capacity to service their obligations is not based upon explicit corporate assets whose anticipated earning power is sufficient to cover interest, dividend, and principal payments as they come due. Rather, market estimates of these firms' debt-service capacity is based upon the expectation of a taxpayer bailout of FSLIC.

This expectation, though basically correct, is not yet entirely nailed down. A destabilizing characteristic of the current situation is that the financial machinery to effect the anticipated bailout is not fully in place. The incompleteness of bailout arrangements encourages doubts about the timeliness and adequacy of authorities' response to whatever crises might develop. In turn, these doubts simultaneously: (1) raise the interim cost of financing FSLIC debt and FSLIC-guaranteed deposits and (2) encourage the public to test FSLIC's debt-servicing capacity at irregular intervals. Each of these tests creates a situation that authorities could easily misplay into a crisis. In parallel situations in several individual states (e.g., Mississippi, Ohio, and Maryland) during the last 15 years, when serious misplays have occurred, a bureaucratic meltdown of state-sponsored deposit-insurance funds has followed. These meltdowns have caused inconvenience and sometimes explicit losses to depositors in insured thrifts.

THE POLICY IMPASSE: THE SIREN SONG OF PROCRASTINATION

The policy problem facing Congress and the Bush administration is threefold. First, they must shore up the explicit finances of FSLIC. Second, they must give FSLIC or a successor agency a clear and positive obligation to use the resources supplied to recapitalize the assets of zombie and near-zombie thrifts in efficient ways that minimize taxpayer losses properly measured. To establish accountability for the insolvency-resolution process, objective procedures must be developed and promulgated to clarify: (1) how firms are to be targeted for takeover, liquidation, or merger; (2) how cases are to be ordered for resolution; and (3) how to demonstrate that taxpayers are getting full value in each deal. Third, they must reform the federal deposit-insurance system to assure that a new generation of zombie financial institutions does not develop in the future.

The market value of a FSLIC guarantee may be conceived in two ways. Its value to an individual thrift is the capitalized value of the interest saving that the guarantee creates for its deposits and other forms of debt. But for policymakers, the relevant value is the capitalized value of the net costs that supporting the guarantee may be projected to impose on FSLIC and unknown federal taxpayers. This second value should be estimated separately for each thrift and made the focus for insolvency-resolution decisions and future FSLIC budgets. The aggregate value of these guarantees represents the federal government's equity stake in the thrift industry and for policy purposes needs to be recognized explicitly as an equity position and managed as such. For years, the extent of FSLIC's *de facto* nationalization has been disguised by giving confusing names to nontraditional ways of exercising ownership authority. So-called management consignments, consent agreements, net worth certificates, and phoenix, regulatory accounting, and FDIC-takeover programs keep regulators and Congress from confronting honestly and in timely fashion the long-run costs of replacing private capital with imperfectly structured government capital, and of continuing to distort private decisions by a combination of subsidies to risk-taking and expanding bureaucratic intervention. In particular, efforts to expand FSLIC's liquidity through exotic financing instruments such as FSLIC notes, spread-maintenance agreements, and tax breaks for acquirers of failing institutions are misguided in that they simultaneously feed and obfuscate the problems posed by insolvent thrifts.

Repeatedly postponing meaningful reform constitutes a form of legislative and regulatory gambling that imposes two kinds of unnecessary costs on federal taxpayers. Official procrastination has served to increase both the size of FSLIC's accumulated losses and the interest cost to taxpayers of keeping this underwater insurer and its weakest clients in play. FSLIC's accumulated losses have increased because zombie firms face strong incentives to undertake high-risk, all-or-nothing financial plays. On average, these last-ditch maneuvers load expected net losses onto FSLIC and bid down simultaneously the profit margins that their healthy competitors can currently earn and the present discounted value of the future profits that these competitors can reasonably project. The interest cost paid on the debt that FSLIC and its weakest clients float is also driven higher by keeping FSLIC in an undercapitalized state. FSLIC's shortage of explicit financial resources makes institutional lenders (who must be able to establish conformance with a prudent-man standard of performance in the event losses ensue) insist on being compensated even for far-fetched default possibilities inherent in the formal weaknesses and imperfections in the support that FSLIC can command from U.S. Treasury resources. FSLIC, its subsidiaries, and its insured clients all benefit from the widespread conjecture that Congress and the president are highly unlikely to allow FSLIC to default permanently on its promises. Nevertheless, formal and procedural weaknesses in Treasury support of FSLIC and FSLIC's own lack of enterprise-contributed capital undermine the credibility of FSLIC's direct and indirect obligations. This means that these obligations carry somewhat higher interest rates than the market would require them to carry if either FSLIC were adequately recapitalized or FSLIC obligations were formally and fully guaranteed by the U.S. Treasury.

Though costly to taxpayers, procrastination is attractive to federal officials for three primary reasons. First, the budget discipline to which Congress and regulatory bureaus subject themselves is dangerously incomplete. Budget procedures acknowledge the effects of explicit income and expenditures, but fail to account for the implicit revenues and costs properly associated with tax forgivenesses, federal guarantees, and other types of forward and contingent commitments. This loophole in budget discipline distorts government decisions and lessens officials' formal accountability for the long-run economic consequences of their actions. This lack of accountability tempts officials to put off painful adjustments and to gamble. They win their gamble if either they can leave office before the consequences of their procrastination become clear or if an extraordinary turn of economic events (such as a sharp fall in interest rates or a sharp rise in oil prices) should develop that lets the zombies win their bets. By the same token, the worsening problems that officials inherit as deferrals from the past seem to saddle them unfairly with popular blame for the unpleasant consequences of decisions taken in predecessor regimes. Second, officials can reap short-term benefits from not settling things. Explicitly resolving FSLIC's insolvency promises to change the pattern of explicit and implicit taxes and subsidies that currently flow through to various political constituencies. This makes lobbyists eager to influence how the costs of dealing with long-festering insolvencies and deposit-insurance subsidies will finally be distributed across the population of taxpayers. Leaving tough issues open keeps the constituencies that promise to be most affected by a final resolution willing to deliver quasi-extortionary forms of tribute to politicians. They do this in the hopes of influencing regulators and legislators either to avoid solutions particularly unfavorable to them or to promote solutions that they find particularly desirable. Third, most legislators lack the time and expertise to master complex issues. They seek to sort through competing sources of information and disinformation in frankly short-cut ways.

In the case of FSLIC's imbedded losses, it was difficult for a financially unsophisticated observer to isolate the truth in conflicting analyses being offered by congressional staff, outside experts, the deposit-insurance bureaucracy, and industry lobbyists. Practical politicians found it easier to believe practitioners than abstract economic analysts and to believe those who argued for continuing the current situation rather than to rethink completely the costs and benefits of FSLIC insurance. Lobbying activity by bureaucrats and industry leaders made the benefits of recommended changes in financial regulation (such as enforcing capital requirements and adopting market-value accounting for financial institutions) seem both unduly uncertain and to be offset over a possibly prolonged start-up period by foreseeable costs of effecting a transition. The threat of having to live through negative early effects makes postponing needed changes attractive to officials whose decision-making horizons are short, and who may be more than ordinarily sensitive to the embarrassment of having to admit making false starts and reversing them. Appointed and elected officials fear being forced from office for having been prematurely judged to have adopted poor policies. This fear predisposes them to go slow and to put undue weight on the initial effects of changes in public policies.

Saying that procrastination benefits officials in these ways does not imply that officials are fully aware of these benefits or that they calculate them either consciously or routinely. The argument does not purport to get "inside the heads" either of particular federal officials or of the operators of zombie thrifts. Rather, the purpose is to clarify the web of unfortunate incentives that has been thrown off by the objective political, economic, and bureaucratic environments in which these parties operate. These incentives effectively put a high price on doing the "right" things.

The root problem is ignorance, not venality. Government officials and deposit-institution managers are often persons of strong character. Many of them have explicitly resisted the temptations raised by these incentives, while others may not even have stooped to consider them. At the same time, some parties may have responded to elements of these incentives without self-consciously realizing that they were doing so.

The remedy for ignorance is knowledge. Partial or total blindness to the implications of these incentives and their potential costs cannot be deemed either a virtue or an excuse. It is a form of culpable ignorance. Parties who inadequately protect their own wealth or wealth that others directly or indirectly entrust to them effectively tempt others to take that wealth unjustly.

It is said that none are so blind as those who will not see. It is also said that being blind to reason is worse than being blind in sight. This book seeks to open the reader's eyes to the temptations that are raised by the incentives under which federal officials and one set of federally insured deposit institutions currently operate. As long as these incentive defects survive, financial instability threatens.

Chapter Two

RISK, S&L CAPITAL, AND THE FRAMEWORK OF FSLIC REGULATION

Deposit institutions are in an inherently risky business. Managers' ability to pay dividends to stockholders depends on finding ways to earn more on their loans and investments than they need to pay out on average to their guarantors, depositors, and nondeposit creditors. A financial firm expects to earn profits by analyzing risks and trading off increments in recognized risks for increments in anticipated returns.

Deposit institutions take many kinds of risk: credit risk, interest-volatility risk, liquidity risk, affiliated-institution risk, technological risk, regulatory risk, and risks of managerial fraud and incompetence. The details of the contracts a firm signs with its managers, stockholders, depositors, and insurers determine how these risks are shared.

DIFFERENT PROFESSIONS' DEFINITIONS OF AN INDIVIDUAL FIRM'S CAPITAL

Risk exists in any endeavor that can develop losses. Taking risks is part and parcel of the core business activity of a financial institution. Risky loans and investments cannot always turn out favorably. An institution's net worth or capital position determines its intrinsic capacity to fight off the potentially crippling effects of prospective losses. Essentially, a firm's capital is a measure of how much risk its owners stand ready to absorb. The *de facto* economic impact of losses as they begin to develop is to *decapitalize* the firm. In this respect, a firm's capital performs functions for a corporation's debt-holders and guarantors that parallel those fulfilled by a body's immune system. In terms of this biological analogy, profit opportunities may be likened to a firm's lifeblood, which carries helpful items such as oxygen and nutrients (revenues) throughout the body along with harmful germs and waste materials (costs) that it seeks to transport to excretory organs. If germs and poisons overwhelm the immune system, the body either may not survive or may survive only with the help of energetic outside intervention.

As a matter of theory, virtually all observers agree that a firm's capital may be identified as its net worth, which is the difference between the aggregate values of its assets and its nonownership liabilities. Insolvency exists *de facto* when an institution loses the capacity to discharge without outside aid liabilities to nonowners completely and in timely fashion. To an economist, *de facto* insolvency exists when the value of an institution's assets falls short of the value of its nonownership liabilities.

In practice, economists, accountants, and lawyers define insolvency in ways that embody different theories both of how to value assets and liabilities and of what particular assets and liabilities ought to enter into the net-worth equation. Most economists prefer to use market values (i.e., the prevailing prices at which individual items can be bought and sold) and to count as assets and liabilities all sources of positive or negative future cash flows. The accounting profession prefers to enter as any item's "book value" a measure that is based on the historical cost at which the specific position was originally acquired. It has also decided to classify some types of asset or liability positions out of the net-worth equation. Accountants' generally accepted accounting principles (GAAP) designate these positions as unbookable "off-balance-sheet" items, whose value they typically discuss in footnotes to the balance sheets they construct. Finally, lawyers prefer to put especially heavy weight on whether current assets cover current liabilities. In this context, "current" means coming due within the immediate future. Effectively, the legal approach factors elements of liquidity into the solvency calculation.

WHAT IS CAPITAL FOR FSLIC?

In calculating the capital of a corporation such as FSLIC that writes financial guarantees or insurance, in addition to whether to employ market or historical-cost values and to include unbookable as well as bookable sources of income, variations exist in how to conceive and value the contingent liabilities that one may reasonably infer from the coverage the company writes. The value of these liabilities depends critically on the ways that the insurer monitors and disciplines clients who aggressively impose risks on the insurer that may or may not have been fully foreseen when the contract was designed.

Until 1986, FSLIC and GAO selected accounting variations that papered over the ways in which the industry's escalating financial problems were creating reservable losses for FSLIC. Even in 1986 and 1987, FSLIC's imbedded losses were only partially recognized. The basic problem is that one cannot reliably assess the value of a guarantee contract merely by analyzing the outlays the guarantor has been required to make in the past. Instead, the value of the contract must be determined by a financial analysis of the contingencies to which it is subject.

One way to dramatize the FSLIC's apparent corporate insolvency is to think of it as facing a wave of current claims from economically devastated thrift clients. Each of these clients can be compared to a worker who has been injured in the workplace. In some of the claims, something akin to a piece of hazardous financial machinery may be said to have suddenly backfired or malfunctioned, catching the equivalent of the operator's finger, hand, or arm in a chain of cog-wheels. In other cases, we may treat the claimants' jobs as having exposed them for years on end to the equivalent of inadequately controlled, slow-acting health hazards, such as radiation or conta-gious diseases, that have long incubation periods.

FSLIC's current situation has two disastrous features. First, hundreds of severe job-related accidents and illnesses require treatment at the same time. Second, this is occurring in an industry that has assigned all its business to a single insurer whose financial resources and personnel are not sufficient to meet the demands the firm now con-fronts. Hundreds of severely wounded thrifts have been shouldering their way through the doors of emergency treatment centers that their insurer has hurriedly had to set up. Because client needs have over-whelmed both FSLIC's financial resources and the staff available to man its emergency treatment facilities, far too few of its wounded clients have received prompt or adequate treatment.

A good picture of the situation emerges from tables 2-1 and 2-2. Table 2-1 tracks the number of accounting insolvencies and the num-ber of formal insolvency resolutions since 1975. Table 2-2 summa-rizes the record of disciplinary actions taken by FSLIC since 1980. Far from being a completely unforeseeable situation, hundreds of FSLIC clients have been bleeding for years. Instead of routinely re-solving patients' need for medical care, hundreds of them were given the equivalent of blood transfusions or painkillers (supervisory agreements, cease and desist orders, removals of management, etc.)

Table 2-1 NUMBER OF GAAP INSOLVENCIES AND INSOLVENCY
RESOLUTIONS AT FSLIC-INSURED INSTITUTIONS,
1975–88

Year	Insolvencies Resolved by FSLIC	GAAP-Insolvent Institutions
1975	11	17
1976	12	48
1977	10	38
1978	4	38
1979	4	34
1980	32	43
1981	82	85
1982	247	237
1983	70	293
1984	36	445
1985	64	470
1986	80	471
1987	77	515
1988 (June)	130	496
1988	233	364

Sources: Information for 1975–79 and 1988 was collected in 1988 and
1989 by telephone from FHLBB files; 1980–88 (June) information comes
from Barth and Bradley (1988), whose figures differ slightly from and are
presumably more exact than older sources.
Notes: An insolvency resolution is defined as a regulator-induced
cessation of autonomous operations. It includes liquidations, supervisory
mergers or acquisitions, and loose forms of conservatorship such as the
FHLBB's Phoenix and Management Consignment Programs.
GAAP-insolvent institution is defined as an institution whose net worth
is less than or equal to zero under Generally Accepted Accounting
Principles (GAAP).

and sent home again without having their wounds or diseased conditions remedied in any important way. In doing this, the overseers
of the emergency room gambled that these patients would recover
on their own or at least not return for further care until the overseers'
term of office had expired. Moreover, because Congress and FSLIC
did nothing to eliminate the dangers in the financial workplace responsible for the industry's high rate of individual injury and disease,
new cases crowded in alongside the old.

Through 1983, FSLIC examiners focused their investigations more
on regulatory compliance than on assessing an institution's health

Table 2-2 TALLY OF ADMINISTRATIVE INITIATIVES BY FSLIC TO DISCIPLINE INDIVIDUAL S&L MANAGEMENTS, 1980–86

Year	Supervisory Agreements	Cease and Desist Orders	Removals of Management	Consent to Merge Agreements	Number of Investigations Completed by Office of Enforcement	
					Formal	Informal
1980	1	3	1	6	6	10
1981	0	8	2	33	8	6
1982	5	13	6	49	10	10
1983	39	17	21	22	17	15
1984	116	13	22	38	24	20
1985	233	28	22	65	30	30
1986	214	58	48	130	30	25
1987	106	25	44	102	n.a.	n.a.
1988[a]	83	15	26	63	n.a.	n.a.

Source: FHLBB files.
a. Through Sept. 30, 1988
n.a. = not available.

(Strunk and Case, 1988, pp. 120–5). FSLIC examiners conducted their investigations by checklist and rulebook rather than as appraisals. Even when examiners found evidence of serious weakness, FSLIC officials did not set aside sufficient reserves for its loss exposure, even though FSLIC often did not possess sufficient authority or will to correct matters and thus reduce its exposure. Prior to the 1982 Garn-St Germain Act, when a failing client had a state charter, for example, FSLIC officials had to negotiate opportunities for closure and takeover with often resistant state officials. Due-process restrictions designed to protect managers and owners from high-handed regulation put undue burdens of proof on examiners and supervisors. The difficulty of building an appeal proof case for either a cease and desist order or a removal of management led FHLBB officials to emphasize the execution of relatively toothless supervisory agreements over these tougher measures (Strunk and Case, 1988, pp. 115–17 and 121–25). Supervisory agreements could be—and often were—subsequently disregarded by tough-minded or desperate managements.

FSLIC officials were also slow to see the need to expand their field examination staffs. The number of field examiners was allowed to decline in 1982, 1983, and 1984. In 1984, Chairman Gray's already belated decision to budget for a larger force for 1985 was stymied by the Office of Management and Budget (OMB). OMB officials focused on reducing short-run cash outlays. Failing to see FSLIC's implicit losses as the logical equivalent of explicit government spending, they thought they could reduce the federal deficit by refusing to authorize the FHLBB to request an expansion in this staff from Congress. This bureaucratic deadlock was finally broken in July 1985, when the FHLBB transferred its examiners administratively from the Board to the Federal Home Loan Banks, but this effort was both too little and too late.

Years of deferring both the effective treatment of victims and the correction of unsafe working conditions have created the equivalent of a health-care crisis in the thrift industry. This book seeks to take the measure of this crisis: to trace its origins and growth and to clarify what kinds of policy actions would and would not bring the problem under control again. It does this precisely because a policymaker's view of what structural and regulatory reforms are needed depends intimately on his or her view of what went wrong in the first place. After decades of either doing nothing or habitually doing a number of fundamentally wrong things, it is hard for authorities to confront their errors. It is all too tempting to blame the problem wholly on bad or dishonest management at insolvent S&Ls. But misdiagnosing the roots of the problem means being lured down unproductive paths of reform.

THE CAPITAL-ADEQUACY QUESTION

In the case of a thrift whose capital is adequate relative to a given set of business risks, FSLIC has minimal need to reserve for a loss exposure. But this is a deceptively simple statement because the concept of a numerically adequate minimum level of capital for an insured deposit institution is a profoundly confused issue.

It is easy to tell when an insured institution's capital has been judged totally inadequate. We need only to skim the *Wall Street Journal* for notices of FSLIC action to merge, to liquidate, or to take over the firm. However, the procedures by which FSLIC decides whether and when to resolve a given insolvency have not been made clear. The confusion has three dimensions.

First, we must recognize that a deposit insurer contributes *de facto* capital whenever and to the extent that it effectively underprices its guarantees of an institution's debt. The root of this part of the confusion is that uncompensated government decisions to forbear from enforcing capital requirements at insufficiently capitalized firms convert FSLIC guarantees into virtually free government capital. Unless authorities adapt their requirements to force an appropriate recapitalization, the capitalized value of the guarantees the insurer offers increases whenever the enterprise-contributed capital of a firm declines or the riskiness of either its portfolio or its economic environment increases. Clearly, it would be a mistake to count the value of FSLIC-contributed guarantees as part of a thrift's capital for regulatory purposes.

The second source of confusion turns on the need to identify new elements in the evolving set of risks that a thrift's capital is supposed to block out for FSLIC. Government regulators are slow to recognize innovations in the character of relevant risks to which the insurance fund is exposed, and are less attuned to risks of sudden collapse and go-for-broke risk taking than to risks of slow deterioration. The major distinction here is between what we may call endogenous (or client-selected) and exogenous (or uncontrolled) risk. Uncontrolled risk consists of macroeconomic risk, competitive-situation risk, and political/regulatory risk. Client-selected risks may be described as client business or portfolio strategies that impose potential losses on the fund. They include exposure to risks from bad decisions, from insider crime, from subsidiaries and holding-company affiliates, from customer defaults, and from leveraged speculation. We may call these risks, respectively, management-competence risk, management-dishonesty risk, affiliated-firm risk, asset-quality risk, and voluntary interest rate and leverage risk. To guard against client-selected risk, shareholders and/or bank guarantors must engage in loss prevention: monitoring, bonding, and risk-sharing provisions. Default, leverage, and interest rate risks are also partly alleviated by the internal diversification of a firm's portfolio and vary with such elements as the firm's exposure to geographic risks and regulatory or tax changes.

The third source of confusion concerns how to calculate the level of enterprise-contributed capital. This problem has two interconnected subdimensions of its own:

1. Issues of asset and liability recognition;
2. Issues of asset and liability valuation.

Item Recognition. Recognizing whether and how much various assets increase the firm's "cushion against adversity," and how much various liabilities decrease it, is greatly complicated by financial innovation and by clientele pressure on deposit-institution regulators. The main issues are the need to incorporate hard-to-value items that accountants have so far dismissed as unbookable, and the difficulty of handling categories of debt that may be said to include elements of partial ownership. The 1988 international agreement on risk-based capital requirements for commercial banks and a U.S. interagency coordinating group known as the Federal Financial Institutions Examination Council have codified twin concepts of permanent and temporary sources of capital funding into parallel *empirical* definitions of primary and secondary capital, and have developed systems for combining them into a single number. The toughest issues have proved to be whether and how to include:

□ reserves for loan losses;
□ nonownership sources of funding whose contractual repayment streams may be legitimately deferred: convertible debt, intermediate and short-term debt that is subordinated to deposits, preferred stock, and income bonds;
□ unrealized capital gains and losses; and
□ going-concern values.

Item Valuation. Asset and liability values come out differently depending upon how we resolve two fundamental dilemmas in economic measurement:

☐ Do we or do we not adjust an observed time series of item values for the effect of inflation?
☐ Do we use historical cost or current market values as the fundamental measure of value?

Whether or not to adjust for inflation is primarily a matter of whether there is a need to assure comparability in purchasing power over time. Whether to use historical cost or current market values is a more crucial matter, because the decision to make anything but market values the basis for measuring regulatory capital widens opportunities for clients to cook their reported capital in unhealthy ways.

Two problems in measuring deposit-institution capital on a historical-cost basis make this very clear. First, even at the outset, using acquisition cost undervalues an institution's best portfolio decisions and overvalues its worst ones. But second and far worse, not modifying these values to reflect subsequent market developments neglects irrefutable and often readily observed evidence that surfaces over time on the differential value of a firm's investments. The fundamental weakness may be underscored by reciting an apocryphal story about a collector of caesarabilia who impressed everyone he knew by spending over a million dollars to amass an extensive collection of documents bearing the autographs of Roman emperors.

Late in his life, the collector decided to donate his documents to a famous university. However, experts called in to appraise the collection gave him some unpleasant news. They found that his collection consisted almost entirely of forgeries. Citing the high prices he had paid in acquiring his collection, he naturally challenged their finding. Unfortunately for him, the experts could prove conclusively that, no matter whose signature might be inked at the bottom, it was not reasonable to believe that documents composed in modern English could have been written by a Roman emperor.

Moral: The moral of this story is *not* just that confidence men exist. It is that guarantors, depositors, and stockholders should not be as naive as this collector was about the economic relevance of the *acquisition costs* of deposit-institution assets and liabilities. An institution's loan and investment successes and failures need to be checked and appraised on an ongoing basis by objective experts, using up-to-date records of prices observed in comparable transactions.

BACKGROUND SUMMARY OF INDUSTRY PROBLEMS AND FEDERAL GOVERNMENT RESPONSES

During the last 25 years, U.S. thrift institutions have faced a difficult competitive environment. Competitive pressure forced thrift institutions to become much fewer in number, while economies of large-scale production and distribution forced them to become much bigger in average size. Between 1960 and 1987, the number of thrift institutions chartered as savings associations more than halved (from 6,320 to 2,961) and the health of 25 percent of the survivors became highly questionable. Over the same period, aggregate assets at FSLIC-insured firms grew from $67.4 billion to $1,251.6 billion. The decline in numbers was less rapid for the sum of FSLIC-insured S&Ls *and* savings banks (from 4,098 to 3,147), while the number of FDIC-insured savings banks actually increased (from 325 to 485). Besides differences in individual-firm entry and exit, these differential trends reflect conversions of S&Ls to savings banks, the decline of state-sponsored funds for insuring deposits at state-chartered thrifts, and the recent weakening in the perceived strength of FSLIC guarantees relative to those of the FDIC.

These trends reflect a treacherous economic environment that generated swings in inflation and interest rates and in individual-firm technologies, income, and net worth. The combination of circumstances put the economic survival of many individual firms and the careers of many individual thrift managers squarely on the line. Hard times for the thrift industry meant hard times for its government regulators and insurers. Over this same interval, several state-sponsored deposit-insurance schemes for thrifts became formally bankrupt, while accumulated and projected losses imposed on FSLIC became increasingly severe. Economists can demonstrate that FSLIC's net reserves were negative throughout the 1970s and 1980s. As shown in chapter one, table 1-1, however, government estimates did not judge FSLIC to be officially insolvent until 1986.

A chronicle of major federal laws affecting savings institutions since 1932 is shown in table 2-3. The period since 1970 provides evidence of alternating congressional concern for readjusting the pattern of federal regulation and taxation to help or to rein in savings institutions. Between 1968 and 1974, federal legislation sought primarily to assist thrifts by maintaining differential deposit-rate ceilings, by expanding their mortgage-lending powers, and by making it easier for them to resell the mortgages they originated. Between 1974 and 1980, in contrast, except for maintaining differential deposit-rate ceilings, Congress did little to assist thrifts. Legislation focused predominantly on protecting household customers from being discriminated against by deposit-institution lenders. In 1980 and 1982 the pendulum swung again, with legislation aimed at jettisoning deposit-rate ceilings seeking to help thrift institutions by radically extending their range of permissible activities. Since 1984, austerity has reasserted itself. Effective income tax rates have increased for many thrift institutions and new restrictions on thrift operations have been introduced.

Regulatory changes tell a similar story. Evidence of the flow of concern exercised by the industry's inherently sympathetic chief federal regulator, the Federal Home Loan Bank Board (FHLBB), appears in table 2-4. The 1981 to 1983 changes in FHLBB regulation may be said to have expanded opportunities for thrifts to take risks; 1984 changes had a mixed impact on thrifts' risk-taking potential; but since 1985, changes have tended to limit thrifts' risk-taking authority.

Against this triple-threat background of economic adversity, expanding technological opportunities, and changing government attitudes and rules, individual thrift failures may be seen to have multiple causes. These causes may be summarized in terms of investment or funding strategies and tactics that proved unfortunate. Of course, whenever an analyst knows how a particular regulatory or investment play eventually turned out, he or she must take care to avoid the information contamination inherent in Monday morning quarterbacking. In any economic postmortem of managerial performance, the key is to identify the reasons a troubled firm adopted its fatal strategies and tactics in the first place, and to evaluate the reasonableness and integrity of the managerial decision processes that underlay them at the time they were made.

INCENTIVE CONFLICTS BETWEEN FSLIC AND INSOLVENT CLIENTS: THE WISDOM OF THROWING THE LONG BALL

Economic analysis indicates that both the *timing* and *distribution* of losses suffered by stockholders and FSLIC are very different from what ordinary accounting records show. When things go wrong, accounting records tend to lag the true decline in value. All sour loans look bad once the underlying projects collapse, but loans collateralized by collapsing projects start losing value long before the project goes completely to pieces.

Table 2-3 MAJOR FEDERAL LAWS AFFECTING THE SAVINGS INSTITUTION BUSINESS, 1932–87

Date	Law	Key Provisions
1932	Federal Home Loan Bank Act	Established the Federal Home Loan Banks under the supervision of the Federal Home Loan Bank Board to provide a central credit facility for home financing institutions.
1933	Banking Act	Created the Federal Deposit Insurance Corporation to insure demand and time deposits at commercial banks and savings banks.
1933	Home Owners' Loan Act	Authorized the creation under the Federal Home Loan Bank Board (FHLBB) of a system of federally chartered and supervised savings and loan associations.
1934	National Housing Act	Established the Federal Savings and Loan Insurance Corporation to insure savings accounts at member associations; created the Federal Housing Administration to insure mortgage and other loans made by private lenders.
1944	Servicemen's Readjustment Act (The G.I. Bill of Rights)	Established a program of loan guarantees under Veterans Administration auspices to encourage private lending on generous terms to veterans of the armed forces.
1949	Housing Act	Established national housing goals of "a decent home and suitable living environment for every American family"; provided grants to municipalities for public housing and slum clearance; set up a program of financial assistance for rural areas under the Farmers Home Administration.
1961	Housing Act	Authorized new programs for federal involvement in housing, including subsidized rental housing for low- and moderate-income families; expanded funding for FNMA special assistance functions.
1968	Housing and Urban Development Act	Gave federal associations the authority to invest in mobile home and home equipment loans; expanded their authority to issue a wide variety of savings plans, notes, bonds and debentures.

1970	Emergency Home Finance Act	Created the Federal Home Loan Mortgage Corporation, under the FHLBB, to provide a secondary market for conventional, FHA, and VA mortgages.
1974	Housing and Community Development Act	Liberalized the types and amounts of loans a federal association may make.
1974	Equal Credit Opportunity Act	Prohibited discrimination in credit transactions on the basis of sex or marital status.
1974	Real Estate Settlement Procedures Act	Provided comprehensive guidelines for loan closing costs and settlement practices.
1975	Home Mortgage Disclosure Act	Required most financial institutions to disclose the number and dollar amount of mortgage loans made, by geographical area.
1976	Tax Reform Act	Reduced certain allowable federal income tax deductions for savings institutions and increased the minimum tax rate; liberalized IRA and Keogh account provisions.
1977	Housing and Community Development Act	Liberalized association lending limits; required financial institution regulatory agencies to take into account an institution's record of serving the credit needs of its community when evaluating applications for new facilities, mergers, and other matters.
1978	Financial Institutions Regulatory and Interest Rate Control Act	Increased FDIC and FSLIC insurance limits for IRA and Keogh accounts from $40,000 to $100,000; provided for FHLBB chartering of federal savings banks; amended Consumer Credit Protection Act establishing rights and responsibilities for electronic funds transfers.

Table 2-3 Continued

Date	Law	Key Provisions
1980	Depository Institutions Deregulation and Monetary Control Act	Shifted deposit account authority from individual depository institution regulators to a newly created Depository Institution Deregulation Committee (DIDC); increased FSLIC and FDIC insurance for all accounts from $40,000 to $100,000; gave the Federal Reserve authority to set reserve requirements on short-term accounts at all depository institutions; extended the federal override of state usury ceilings on various loans; authorized NOW accounts nationwide.
1982	Garn-St Germain Depository Institutions Act	For all depository institutions, preempted or severely limited state due-on-sale clause and alternative mortgage loan restrictions; granted broader powers to the federal deposit insurance corporations; mandated the phase-out of the savings interest rate differential by 1/1/84. For insured institutions with deficient net worth, provided for FSLIC and FDIC assistance to bring net worth to required levels, in the form of insurance corporation notes exchanged for net worth certificates issued by the institution. For savings institutions, eased charter and conversion limits. For federal associations, created or expanded lending and investment authority; authorized the acceptance of demand deposits from business and agricultural loan customers; removed mortgage loan-to-value ratio limits.
1984	Deficit Reduction Act	Reduced the tax benefits from certain corporate tax preference items; simplified tax credit rules; extended the tax exemption for qualified mortgage subsidy bonds; phased out graduated tax rates for large corporations; created new reporting procedures for mortgage interest, property foreclosure or abandonment, and IRAs.
1984	Comprehensive Crime Control Act	Prohibited financial institution employees from accepting anything of value from anyone in connection with any transaction or business dealing.

1986	Bank Bribery Amendments Act	Clarified that actions in violation of the "Bank Bribery" statute are limited to those which are based on intent to corrupt.
1986	Tax Reform Act	Reduced top corporate tax rate from 46% to 34% and also reduced the percentage-of-taxable-income bad-debt deduction from 40% to 8%; provided for three-year carrybacks and 15-year carryforwards for savings institution net operating losses; extended to eight years the carryover period for net operating losses incurred in taxable years beginning after December 31, 1981, and before January 1, 1986.
1986	Money Laundering Control Act	Created a new federal crime of money laundering, exposing financial institutions to new liability for involvement in money-laundering transactions. Also established a new Bank Secrecy Act offense to prohibit structuring any transaction in a manner which causes a financial institution not to file required reports.
1987	Competitive Equality Banking Act	Authorized a $10.8 billion "recapitalization" bonding program for FSLIC. Approved supervisory forbearance of up to three years for well-managed, capital-weak institutions in economically depressed areas. Established a schedule to phase out special FSLIC premium assessments; provided for balance sheet recovery of FSLIC secondary reserves. Approved one-year moratorium, with "stiff" exit fees thereafter for conversions from FSLIC to FDIC insurance. Reaffirmed sense-of-Congress resolution purporting to hold federal "full faith and credit" backing for insured deposits. Limited check-holds and mandated caps for adjustable rate mortgages, home equity loans. Authorized nondepository firm purchases of institutions with assets of $500 million or more. Set chartering, growth limits for nonbank banks. Simplified restructuring of troubled loans and maximization of recoveries of these loans.

Source: United States League of Savings Institutions, *1987 and 1988 Savings Institution Sourcebooks.*

Table 2-4 MAJOR REGULATORY CHANGES AFFECTING SAVINGS INSTITUTIONS 1981–87

Date Effective	Item	Provisions
Jan. 1981	Trust powers	Federal associations may offer trust services under regulations comparable to those for national banks.
Jan. 1981	Debit cards	Federal associations may issue debit cards which permit savers to make withdrawals and nontransferable third-party payments directly to merchants and others.
Jan. and Aug. 1981	Remote service units (RSUs)	Federal associations may not install RSUs without prior FHLBB approval or geographic restrictions.
Feb. 1981	Outside borrowing	FSLIC members may now borrow from sources outside the FHLB System under much more liberal rules than formerly.
Mar. 1981	Mutual funds	Federal associations may now invest in mutual funds, subject to limits related to the kinds of investments the fund makes.
Apr. 1981	Money market certificate (MMC) rate ceilings	Associations may now offer MMCs and small saver certificates at the new rate on the day after the announcement of Treasury auction results (instead of three days later).
Apr. 1981	Adjustable mortgage loans (AMLs)	Federal associations may now make AMLs subject to regulatory limits relating to consumer protection, under the terms and conditions that best suit borrower and lender needs.
Apr. 1981	Service corporations	Federal association service corporations may now engage in a greatly enlarged list of activities without prior approval; may deal with a broader range of customers; and may borrow subject to fewer restrictions than formerly.
July 1981	Futures transactions	FSLIC members may now deal in a broad range of futures contracts under liberalized investment limits; former eligibility requirement for such transactions have been removed.
July 1981	Graduated payment adjustable mortgage loans	Federal associations may now make adjustable mortgage loans where monthly payments during the first 10 years are less than sufficient to amortize the loan during the full contract period.

Aug. 1981	Savings account rate ceilings	FSLIC members may now issue fixed-term savings accounts with variable interest rates; may pay interest in the form of discounts on savings accounts not subject to rate ceilings; are no longer subject to a 12% ceiling on certificates with terms of 30 months to four years.
Aug. 1981	FHLB advances	FHLB members may now borrow from their district Bank up to the lesser of (a) their legal maximum borrowing limit or (b) 50% of assets.
Oct. 1981	All Savers certificate	Between 10/1/81 and 12/31/81, associations may issue a one-year savings certificate in a minimum denomination no greater than $500, at an interest rate equal to 70% of the annual investment yield on 52-week Treasury bills, the interest on which is tax-exempt up to a once-in-a-lifetime total of $1,000 on an individual federal income tax return ($2,000 on a joint return).
Oct. 1981	Balloon payment mortgage loans	Federal associations may now make nonamortized or partially amortized loans for loan-to-value ratios up to 95% and for terms in excess of five years, at adjustable interest rates.
Oct. 1981	Reverse annuity mortgage loans	Federal associations may make mortgage loans that provide for a stream of payments to the borrower from the lender under more liberal terms than formerly; periodic interest rate adjustments also are permitted.
Nov. 1981	Interest rate ceilings on Money Market Certificates (MMCs)	Associations may now offer new MMCs at a rate tied to the higher of (a) the most recent six-month Treasury bill auction rate or (b) the average of the four most recent auction rates.
Dec. 1981	Retirement savings accounts	Associations may now issue IRA and Keogh accounts with a minimum 18-month term not subject to any rate ceiling; may accept additions to such accounts without extending the maturity of the certificate.
Feb. 1982	Consumer leasing	FSLIC members may engage in personal property leasing on a basis similar to consumer lending powers.
Feb. 1982	Outside borrowing	FSLIC members may borrow outside the FHLB System without limit on the total amount, collateralization or distribution of maturities; may sell loans with recourse, subject to certain rules.

Table 2-4 Continued

Date Effective	Item	Provisions
April 1982	Manufactured home loans	FSLIC members may make balloon payment, graduated payment, adjustable mortgage and other loans on manufactured homes (mobile homes) or land/home combinations without percentage-of-asset limits; may finance insurance premiums.
April 1982	Savings account rules	FSLIC members may issue in negotiable form any certificate whose rules do not provide otherwise; may charge fees for opening and closing accounts and other services; may issue certificates with no limit on maximum maturity; may issue loophole certificates without limit; may issue Eurodollar certificates with minimum terms of 14 days.
May 1982	91-day money market certificate	FHLB members may issue $7,500 minimum, 91-day accounts paying up to the 91-day Treasury bill rate.
May 1982	3½ year deregulated certificate	FHLB members may issue certificate accounts of less than $100,000 with original maturities of 3½ years or more, not subject to any rate ceiling. No minimum is required, but the account must be offered in a $500 denomination. Additions may be permitted during the first year without extending the maturity.
May 1982	Retail repurchase agreements	FSLIC members may offer retail repurchase agreements without net-worth-based limits, as long as net worth is at least at specified levels.
June 1982	Net worth computation	FSLIC members may exclude from liabilities in computing net worth certain contra-asset accounts, including loans in process, unearned discounts, and deferred fees and credits.
Aug. 1982	Financial options trading	FSLIC members may buy financial options and write call options without position limits, may write put options up to specified limits.
Aug. 1982	Lending regulations	Federal associations may make a broad range of mortgage loans without detailed regulatory limits; loan payment changes may reflect interest or balance changes from an index, a schedule or a formula.

Sept. 1982	7–31 day account	FHLB members may offer $20,000 minimum certificates with a maturity or notice period of 7 to 31 days, paying a rate whose ceiling is tied to the three-month Treasury bill rate.
Sept. 1982	Net worth computations	FSLIC members may count subordinated debt securities, mutual capital certificates and certain other items toward net worth and statutory reserve requirements.
Oct. 1982	Commercial checking account	Federal associations may accept non-interest-bearing demand deposits from any business loan customer; overdraft loans are limited to 5% of assets.
Oct. 1982	Commercial lending	Federal associations may invest up to 40% of assets in loans on commercial real estate; up to 5% of assets in other business or agricultural loans.
Oct. 1982	Consumer loans	Federal associations may invest up to 30% of assets in consumer (non-mortgage) loans.
Oct. 1982	Government NOW account	Federal associations may offer NOW accounts to all levels of government.
Nov. 1982	Appraised equity capital	FSLIC members may include in net worth their appraised equity capital—the difference between book and market value of assets such as land and improvements.
Dec. 1982	Money market account	FHLB members may offer this account without interest rate limits for an initial deposit and average balance of $2,500; no minimum maturity; may have up to six preauthorized transfers per month, but no more than three by draft.
Dec. 1982	Charters	Federal institutions may elect to be chartered as associations or savings banks; state savings banks may obtain federal mutual or stock charters while keeping FDIC insurance.
Dec. 1982	Net worth certificates	Associations with net worth between 0.5% and 3% that meet certain eligibility requirements and agree to specified conditions may issue net worth certificates which, after being exchanged for FSLIC promissory notes, are eligible for inclusion in regulatory net worth.
Jan. 1983	Interest rate ceilings	Ceilings eliminated on short-term accounts with minimum balances of $2,500 or more (7–31 day and super NOW accounts, and 91-day and 26-week MMCs).

Table 2-4 Continued

Date Effective	Item	Provisions
Jan. 1983	Branching	Application process simplified for federal savings institution branches and approval criteria eased.
Feb. 1983	Data processing services	Federal savings institutions may engage in a wider range of data processing activities for themselves, for sale to others, and to provide home banking and other automated services to customers.
Feb. 1983	Net worth certificates (NWCs) and regulatory net worth	FSLIC is committed to buy additional NWCs from an institution once it makes an initial purchase. NWCs that FSLIC is committed to buy may be included in regulatory net worth.
Feb. 1983	FHLB advances	FHLBs may make FSLIC-insured advances to institutions without customary credit evaluations.
Feb. 1983	Deregulated account interest rates	Institutions may negotiate rates, offer rate bonuses or choose any index for rate changes on deregulated deposits.
Feb. and April 1983	Conversions to stock charter	Mutual institutions now have more leeway in structuring and streamlining conversion operations.
March 1983	Grandfathered savings bank powers	State savings banks that convert to federal savings institution charters may continue to exercise the powers they had under the state charter.
April 1983	2½ year certificates	Certificates of 2½ years or more are not subject to interest rate ceilings and minimum balance requirements.
April 1983	Branching	Savings institution branches now are permitted on military installations.
April 1983	Reporting to Federal Reserve	Reporting requirements are eased for depository institutions with reservable liabilities of $2.1 million or less.
May 1983	Loan-to-value ratios	Specific loan-to-value ratios for various types of secured loans are eliminated from the regulations.
May 1983	Due-on-sale clauses	Federal law preempts any state law restricting lenders' rights to exercise due-on-sale clauses.

Date	Topic	Description
July 1983	Savings account loans	Interest rates charged must be at least 1% more than the rate at which the account earns, including the effects of compounding.
Sept. 1983	FHLB advances	FHLBs may make advances for terms of up to 20 (formerly 10) years.
Sept. 1983	Charters and bylaws	Streamlined regulations provide one stock and one mutual charter form for federal savings institutions, and bylaw guidelines rather than prescribed bylaws.
Oct. 1983	Deposit rate ceilings	Interest rate ceilings are eliminated on deposits with maturities or notice periods of more than 31 days and on deposits of at least 7 days with $2,500 minimum balances.
Dec. 1983	IRA and Keogh account minimums	Minimum balance requirements are eliminated for any class of account containing IRA or Keogh funds.
Dec. 1983	Applications for FSLIC insurance	Minimum capital requirements raised, other restrictions imposed on institutions seeking FSLIC insurance.
Jan. 1984	Deposit account ceilings	The minimum amount for deposits that are exempt from interest rate ceilings is reduced from $2,500 to $1,000.
Jan. 1984	Transaction account reserves	Depository institutions must hold 3% reserves against the first $28.9 (formerly $26.3) million of net balances and 12% against balances over that figure.
Feb. 1984	Bank holding companies	Nonbanking activities are added to the permissible list and certain application procedures are simplified.
July 1984	Finance subsidiaries	Federal associations may establish finance subsidiaries to issue securities for the parent institution.
July 1984	Interest rate risk management	Insured institutions must establish policies for the management of interest rate risk in the institutions' operations.
Aug. 1984	Management of new institutions	In order to obtain FSLIC insurance, newly organized institutions must meet strict requirements to avoid director and management conflicts of interest and protection of corporate opportunity.
Aug. 1984	Acquisitions of converted institutions	Changes in control of the stock of newly converted insured institutions are restricted for a period of three years.

Table 2-4 Continued

Date Effective	Item	Provisions
Sept. 1984	Net worth certificates	The initial assistance level is raised and certain requirements were simplified for FSLIC's program of assistance to member institutions.
Sept. 1984	Corporate name and advertising	Names and advertising must reflect the savings institution charter status of federal associations and savings banks.
Oct. 1984	Earnings-based accounts (EBAs)	EBAs that conform to specified limitations are FSLIC insured.
Nov. 1984	Remote service facilities	Application procedures are simplified for remote service facilities of FDIC-insured banks.
Dec. 1984	Securities activities	FDIC-insured nonmember banks may underwrite securities and offer brokerage services through separate affiliates.
Dec. 1984	Statements of condition	Annual statement of condition rules are simplified for federal savings institutions.
Jan. 1985	Money market deposit accounts	Minimum required balance is reduced from $2,500 to $1,000.
Jan. 1985	Changes in Keogh, corporate, and other qualified plans	IRS issues new survivor annuity rules to protect the rights of spouses of married participants in qualified plans.
Mar. 1985	Net worth requirements	FSLIC-insured institutions must increase net worth reserves depending on rate of growth. Institutions with more than $100 million in assets must seek permission from the FHLBB to grow faster than 25% a year. Greater new worth is required for institutions with direct investments. Also gradually eliminates the five-year averaging used to calculate net worth levels. Instead, levels must be calculated and met based on a "snapshot" of each institution's asset size at the end of every quarter.

Date	Topic	Description
Mar. 1985	Direct investments	Creates a process of supervisory review and approval of certain types of direct investments in equity securities, real estate and subsidiary companies by FSLIC-insured savings institutions. Also requires institutions to post a 10% reserve against all direct investments made after December 10, 1984, but only if such investments exceed the greater of 10% of the institution's assets or twice its regulatory net worth.
Oct. 1985	Distribution of adjustable rate mortgage (ARM) information	FSLIC-insured institutions must provide all ARM applicants a copy of the Federal Reserve/Federal Home Loan Bank Board's "Consumer Handbook on Adjustable Rate Mortgages" or its equivalent.
Oct. 1985	Loan prepayment penalty	Under certain conditions, prohibits lender from imposing prepayment penalties with respect to loans on the security of borrower-occupied homes.
Dec. 1985	Loan classification of assets	Permits examiners of FSLIC-insured savings institutions to classify questionable loans and other assets for the purposes of requiring general and specific reserve allocations.
Jan. 1986	Credit practices	Covers consumer as well as certain equity mortgage and manufactured (mobile) home loans. Prohibits the use of certain contract provisions and the pyramiding of late charges, and requires that potential cosigners receive notice of consumer credit obligations.
Jan. 1986	Deposit account ceilings lifted	The $1,000 minimum requirement on the money market deposit account, super NOW account, and 7- to 31-day account is eliminated. The 5.25% interest rate ceiling on the NOW account is also lifted.
Jan. 1986	Mortgage interest reporting	Savings institutions must furnish reports to mortgage payers from whom they receive $600 or more of mortgage interest per year. Institutions also must provide this information to the IRS.
Mar. 1986	Interest rate ceilings lifted	The 5.5% ceiling on passbook accounts is lifted. Final phase of savings deregulation is completed. DIDC is terminated.
Mar. 1986	Self-directed retirement plans	Savings institutions are empowered to offer self-directed retirement plans without applying expanded trust powers.

Table 2-4 Continued

Date Effective	Item	Provisions
Oct. 1986	Loan record keeping requirements amended	The FHLBB expands the kind of transactions and loan types that must meet minimum documentation and record keeping requirements. The previous regulation covered only requirements for loans secured by real estate. The amended regulation also requires savings institutions to establish records for commercial and consumer loans.
Jan. 1987	Final rules on regulatory capital and liability growth requirements	FHLBB issues extensive amendments to its 1985 net worth requirements. In order to build regulatory capital to strengthen institutions and protect the FSLIC, required levels of capital will be raised over time from 3% to 6% of liabilities. Each institution's level of capital as of December 31, 1986, and the savings institution business' future return on assets will help determine minimum capital ratios.
April 1987	Compliance with reporting requirements for cash transactions amended	Required savings institutions to establish procedures to assure compliance with Bank Secrecy Act record keeping and reporting requirements; act requires institutions to file currency transaction reports for cash transactions of more than $10,000.
April 1987	Extension of restrictions on direct investments	New regulations require principal supervisory agent preapproval threshold for institutions in compliance with regulatory capital minimums. Institutions with 6% or greater intangible capital have a supervisory threshold for direct investments of three times their tangible capital. Any institution making direct investments at or above the 20% level, however, must notify its principal supervisory agent.
Dec. 1987	Appraisal policies and practices	Sets broad guidelines for savings institutions and service corporation managers and boards to formally adopt "prudent" appraisal policies; requires that appraisals be based on market value, be presented in narrative form and be conducted by qualified appraisers. Institutions are also required to review appraiser performance.

Dec. 1987	Classification of assets rules amended	FHLBB broadens scope of classification system to include all assets of insured savings institutions. Institutions must classify own assets regularly and make quarterly reports on classified assets; must also set aside valuation allowances for possible losses resulting from problem loans.
Dec. 1987	Final rules on individual regulatory capital requirements, capital directives and capital forbearance	FHLBB delegates authority to principal supervisory agents to establish increased individual capital requirements for FSLIC-insured savings institutions on a case-by-case basis; FHLBB may issue capital directives to any insured institution that fails to meet regulatory capital requirements. Regulation establishes a revised policy to extend capital forbearance to well-managed and viable institutions in economically depressed areas.
Dec. 1987	Final rules on uniform accounting standards	FHLBB amends definition of regulatory capital and accounting principles and procedures regulations to bring savings institution accounting standards more in line with those used by banks. Institutions must eventually report virtually all components of regulatory capital in accordance with generally accepted accounting principles or bank-employed regulatory accounting practices.
Dec. 1987	Loan fee accounting	Financial Accounting Standards Board's new rule for loan fee accounting takes effect for fiscal years beginning after December 15. Nonrefundable loan fees and certain direct loan origination costs, net of fees, must be deferred over a loan's life.
Dec. 1987	Qualified thrift lender test	FHLBB establishes a new qualified thrift lender test under which savings institutions must maintain housing-related investments equal to 60% of tangible assets; reduces access to FHLB advances for institutions that fail to meet the Qualified Thrift Lender (QTL) test.
Dec. 1987	Troubled debt restructuring	Authorizes savings institutions to restructure and maximize recoveries on troubled debt under accounting provisions of Financial Accounting Standards Board.

Source: United States League of Savings Association, *1982–1988 Savings Institution Sourcebooks.*

At the same time, it is unfair to analyze a lender's *initial* selection of risk-reward tradeoffs by drawing on information that was not available when its loans and investments were made. In assessing whether the manager of an insolvent or decapitalized thrift acted ineptly or cleverly, the issue is whether the managers made a series of loan deals and securities investments that were certifiably bad at the very moment they were made. Did or did not zombie managers contract for rewards proportionate to the risks assumed? Did or did not these financial plays increase the value of the firms' stock?

Ironically, far from being harmed, managers and stockholders in zombie and near-zombie thrifts typically benefit from placing funds into risky loans and investments at the specific time these commitments are made. However, they do so at the expense of FSLIC and the unknown federal taxpayers who wittingly or unwittingly stand behind FSLIC. Managers and stockholders benefit because taking on new risk increases the aggregate market value of FSLIC's guarantees of any decapitalized firm's deposits. Typically, the aggregate value of a zombie firm's stock jumps in the months immediately after an insolvent firm embarks on a high risk strategy to "grow" its way out of its insolvency. This indicates that financial analysts and outside investors approve of decapitalized firms' adopting an investment strategy of expanding their bets and going for broke. Such a strategy is implemented by attracting additional funds with well-publicized offers of above-market interest rates, and placing the funds thus raised into high-risk, high-yield assets such as junk bonds or speculative real estate and construction ventures.

An indication of this process is shown in table 2-5. A firm's market capitalization is the market value of its stock. This may be calculated as the product of the number of shares outstanding and the price per share. Because data on outstanding shares have been centralized for only a few thrift institutions, it is not possible to construct a representative sample of the response of thrifts' market capitalization to their asset growth. Instead, table 2-5 reports the mean market value of the stock and mean total assets for the 32 thrifts for which two colleagues, Haluk Unal and James Barth, could construct 10 calendar quarters of data, covering 1984.1 to 1986.2. Because other forms of recapitalization are not controlled, the comparison is indicative only. Over these 10 quarters, an increase of 44 percent in mean assets is associated with a 135 percent increase in the mean value of market capitalization.

It is important to understand that FSLIC is damaged and thrift shareholders are enriched by the risky financial plays made by a

Table 2-5 COMPARISON OF MEAN MARKET CAPITALIZATION WITH
MEAN ASSET SIZE FOR 32 SELECTED THRIFT
INSTITUTIONS, 1984–86, BY QUARTER ($ million)

Quarter	Mean Market Capitalization	Mean Total Assets
1984.1	41.5	1,552.2
1984.2	38.2	1,676.9
1984.3	40.9	1,757.0
1984.4	44.3	1,867.7
1985.1	51.4	1,901.4
1985.2	62.7	1,918.7
1985.3	58.0	1,993.2
1985.4	71.6	2,060.9
1986.1	92.5	2,109.3
1986.2	97.3	2,232.7

Source: Analysis of data from FHLBB, Office of Policy and Economic
Research.

decapitalized client, irrespective of whether or not that risky play
later succeeds. The damage develops from the asymmetric distribution of the returns from letting the client use government money
to deal itself in for high stakes at the financial equivalent of regional
or national gaming tables. Of course, if the client wins big, FSLIC
wins something too. The rub lies in allowing the managers of decapitalized firms to claim their salaries during the period the bets
remain on the table and in allowing the firms' stockholders to keep
a larger portion of whatever net or interim winnings accrue than is
justified by their true costs of making the investment. The root problem is that the actuarial value of stockholders' net potential winnings
increases directly with the riskiness of the financial play their firm
makes and decreases with the amount of enterprise-contributed capital they bring to the gaming table. The extreme case is the zombie
firm that brings no capital at all. Such a firm saddles all risk of future
losses on FSLIC, while enjoying at least the possibility of reaping
substantial gains.

Simply stated, a guarantor is exposed to being taken advantage of
by strategic adjustments made by whatever entity it chooses to guarantee. Any defects in the guarantor's systems for measuring, monitoring, and disciplining client risk taking create loopholes whereby
the person or corporation whose debt is guaranteed can adapt its
behavior in hard-to-foresee ways to shift more and different risks

onto the guarantor than the guarantor intended to underwrite. Whether or not the guaranteed entity ever defaults on its debt in a way that later produces explicit monetary damage, the guarantor loses in the sense that the market value at which its side of the guarantee contract could be sold falls at the instant the guaranteed party begins to exploit the loophole.

After a client fails, FSLIC sometimes sues the managers for damages. In looking at a failed institution's investments after the fact, it is important to see that, unless malfeasance and fraud occurred in the process, making risky loans and investments damaged FSLIC not as receiver, but as *insurer*. Managers did not need dishonestly to "rig" their firm's stock. It was enough to produce valuable claims to future income whose value could, and in fact probably did, deteriorate quickly. The damage to FSLIC and federal taxpayers was inflicted by FSLIC's own inadequate systems for managing and pricing client risk. FSLIC procedures shot itself and federal taxpayers in the foot. Like it or not, FSLIC officials and their congressional overseers now face political consequences from having contributed to the wounds.

Any guarantor and its clients face an unavoidable incentive conflict. For this reason, every outside guarantor has a responsibility to protect its capital in two ways. The first is by setting up adequate information and monitoring systems. The second is by undertaking to police client activities in ways that reduce the extent to which its own net worth is exposed to losses brought about by risks that its clients may undertake in their own self-interest. In the face of increasing interest rates, fluctuating real estate prices, and 1980 and 1982 statutory changes in an S&L's financial powers, FSLIC was slow to adapt its oversight procedures to the changing realities of its position in the marketplace.

FSLIC had both the right and the fiduciary duty to criticize client appraisal practices, internal controls, review practices, and loan-selection practices on an ongoing basis. As the economy became more volatile and as the 1980 and 1982 financial-reform acts expanded individual thrifts' risk-taking capacities, FSLIC should have greatly tightened its monitoring of client capital and balance-sheet positions (Kane 1981 and 1982). This is because, as already noted, the asymmetry of FSLIC's participation in client gains and losses rises as the client's business becomes more volatile and as the client's capital position deteriorates. To explain this asymmetry, one may liken client capital to the amount of the deductible applicable to client losses under a casualty insurance policy. The key idea is that a firm's losses cannot directly reach FSLIC until they exceed the value of stockholder capital.

Exercising new portfolio powers granted by the 1980 and 1982 financial reform acts, many deposit-institution managers (particularly at firms that had previously been allowed to become undercapitalized) voluntarily pursued new and (for FSLIC) dangerous forms of financial risk taking. Some of them were taking advantage of the fact that FSLIC personnel proved slow to appreciate how much new forms of risk taking were increasing the value of FSLIC guarantees of client debt. These aggressive managers embraced both new and old forms of risk taking as a way to increase the anticipated return on equity capital their firms could offer actual and potential stockholders. Making riskier loans and investments and financing these activities in riskier fashion increased a thrift's projected interest margin on the funds it raised. It also increased the risk that the firm would become economically insolvent.

In responding to these incentives, it would be a mistake to claim that the managers of decapitalized institutions intended for their firm to fail. They no more intended for their firm to fail than a burgled householder who was perfectly insured against losses from theft would have intended for his or her households goods to be stolen. The critical point is that, when insured households that install burglar alarms or heavy-duty locks are offered no compensating reductions in their insurance premiums, their interest in installing costly alarm systems and hard-to-burgle locks is economically attenuated.

POLITICAL ROOTS AND ECONOMIC EFFECTS OF CAPITAL FORBEARANCE EXTENDED IN THE MID-1980s

As already discussed, during the early 1980s, FHLBB regulators (with behind-the-scenes congressional encouragement and approval) explicitly acceded to industry pressure to lower effective requirements for minimum net worth at decapitalized institutions. In urging this action, industry spokespersons portrayed troubled thrifts as innocent victims whose net-worth positions had been undermined by macroeconomic policies followed by a capricious government. They likened efforts to require decapitalized thrifts to recapitalize themselves to kicking injured parties that were lying on the ground.

They also lobbied hard for government compassion in the form of capital forbearance, new tax breaks, creative accounting privileges, and expanded portfolio powers. One form of lobbying activity that can be easily documented consists of campaign donations made by trade-association and individual-corporation political action committees, or PACs. Between January 1, 1987 and March 31, 1988, PACs raised roughly $213 million and disbursed $162 million (*American Banker* 1988). During these 15 months, $56.4 million of the disbursements went to candidates seeking election in 1988. Trade associations or corporations in financial services or related industries operated 9 of the 50 highest-contributing PACs. These PACs include those of the National Association of Realtors ($982,115), the National Association of Home Builders[1] ($565,971), the American Bankers Association ($380,900), and the U.S. League of Savings Associations ($252,250).

It is generally acknowledged that PACs are less interested in influencing the outcome of particular elections (in fact, they frequently contribute to opposing candidates) than in possibilities for future political influence that their money may buy (Stern 1988). For this reason, senior members of House and Senate Banking Committees, who may be counted upon to sit on the 10-person Conference Committees that determine the final form of deposit-institution legislation, can (if they choose) raise substantial amounts of PAC funds. The February 7, 1989 *Wall Street Journal* summarized the top beneficiaries during the 1984, 1986, and 1988 electoral cycles of 163 PACs sponsored by FSLIC-insured thrift institutions and their trade associations (see table 2-6). Nearly $4.5 million went to House and Senate candidates from the thrift-sponsored PACs during these six years. In addition to this, it must be remembered that thrift-industry executives make personal contributions, finance appearance fees or honoraria for speaking engagements, and participate in fund-raisers of various sorts.

Lobbyists' ability to influence the leading members of oversight committees and subcommittees might be lessened by requiring a public reporting of all activities undertaken by representatives and managers of insured institutions that might be construed as increasing their ability to influence legislative or regulatory decisions. By reducing the advantages of incumbency for those who take substantial amounts of industry funds, such reports could increase congressional turnover where it is most needed, without going so far as to fix for each house a maximum number of years of service parallel to the two-term limit set for the president.

It is true that federal regulations require even zombie institutions to "maintain safe and sound financial policies." But it is obvious

Table 2-6 TOP BENEFICIARIES FROM S&L PAC DONATIONS

Current House and Senate Members who got most from S&L PACs,
1983–88
(Banking Committee member in boldface)

House	
Richard Lehman (D., Calif.)	**$ 49,669**
David Dreier (R., Calif.)	**49,528**
Norman Shumway (R., Calif.)	**43,696**
Bill Lowery (R., Calif.)	42,832
Carroll Hubbard (D., Ky.)	**37,375**
Esteban Torres (D., Calif.)	**37,032**
Richard Gephardt (D., Mo.)	30,631
Frank Annunzio (D., Ill.)	**29,660**
Stephen Neal (D., N.C.)	**27,200**
Mel Levine (D., Calif.)	25,750
Senate	
Pete Wilson (R., Calif.)	$105,409
Robert Dole (R., Kans.)	78,250
Alan Cranston (D., Calif.)	**71,400**
Donald Riegle (D., Mich.)	**66,601**
Slade Gorton (R., Wash.)	56,900
Lloyd Bentsen (D., Tex.)	46,244
Alfonse D'Amato (R., N.Y.)	**39,400**
John Heinz (R., Pa.)	**30,150**
Jake Garn (R., Utah)	**30,050**
Bob Graham (D., Fla.)	**26,450**

Source: Jackson (1989), based on a *Wall Street Journal* tabulation of
Federal Election Commission data.

that regulators cannot enforce so vague a regulation. Even Jehovah
found the need to specify 10 commandments rather than to ask the
Israelites merely to do good and avoid evil. The logical basis for
bringing supervisory actions such as cease and desist orders is precisely the need to establish under due process that a particular activity is unsafe or unsound.

A conscientious manager of a decapitalized thrift finds himself in
a position very much like that of a professional basketball player. A
rulebook exists with which he is supposed to be familiar, yet in
practice what he must obey is not his own interpretation of these
rules, but the interpretation imposed by the referees assigned by the
league. If a player tries to obey a stricter set of rules than league

referees endeavor to enforce, he risks hurting both his career and the fortunes of his team.

FSLIC and FDIC label institutions as "problems" when their examiners grade them as either a 4 or a 5 on a 5-point rating scale developed jointly by the several federal agencies responsible for supervising and regulating deposit institutions. An institution officially fails when its chartering authority directs it to be liquidated, sold, or merged with another firm. Although a problem classification may trace to noncompliance with specific regulations or to other supervisory problems, it is generally intended that firms be designated as problems before they fail, and as category-4 cases before their capital could be shown to be negative by GAAP accounting. Although FSLIC does not regularly publicize the number of institutions receiving a problem rating, figures for 1980–84 were released as part of a congressional hearing (see table 2-7). We can use these figures to investigate how well the "problems" identified in one year predicted the number of insolvency resolutions and GAAP-insolvent cases to be observed in the following year (see table 2-8). In 1981 and 1982 the pseudo-forecast is remarkably accurate, suggesting that decapitalized firms were either being closed by FSLIC or identified as insolvent by GAAP about as promptly as the examination process could uncover them.

However, legislation passed in 1982 expanded opportunities for decapitalized firms to place large bets on the table in a hurry. As a result, GAAP accounting lost accuracy relative to examination reports. At the same time, lobbying pressure encouraged FSLIC's closing process to slow down.

Zombies' capacity to overstate their capital on a GAAP basis appears to lie largely in three developments: (1) being able to classify what were *de facto* direct investments in real estate as commercial mortgage loans and to book phantom interest receipts as income;[2] (2) being able to book as goodwill the capitalized value of deposit-insurance benefits that become impounded in the purchase premiums paid in an acquisition whose cost exceeds the market value of the tangible assets being acquired; and (3) being able to book the full amount of fees paid at loan origination as current income, without deducting the present value of the future costs of servicing the obligations incurred. These accounting loopholes made or kept fast-growing thrifts GAAP-solvent, no matter how questionable the loans they booked might be.

In deemphasizing examination reports as a basis for requiring the recapitalization of economically decapitalized firms, FSLIC failed to

Table 2-7 NUMBER AND ASSET SIZE OF FSLIC-INSURED INSTITUTIONS WITH YEAR-END EXAMINATION RATINGS OF 4 OR 5, 1980–84

| | | Asset-Size Distribution | | | | | |
| | | Less than $300 Million | | Between $300 Million and $1 Billion | | Over $1 Billion | |
Year	Total No.	No.	Total Assets ($ billion)	No.	Total Assets ($ billion)	No.	Total Assets ($ billion)
1980	159	142	10.9	12	6.5	5	8.0
1981	513	427	35.6	63	30.6	23	40.6
1982	720	581	50.5	93	49.5	46	101.2
1983	678	532	50.2	104	53.2	42	98.3
1984	738	544	56.1	141	76.9	53	147.4

Source: Edwin Gray, "Correction of Information Submitted on September 9–10, 1985," submitted to the Banking Committee of the U.S. House of Representatives, September 16, 1985.

Table 2-8 ACCURACY OF FSLIC's 1980–85 YEAR-END EXAMINATION
RATINGS AS PROXY FORECASTS FOR THE NUMBER OF
INSOLVENCY RESOLUTIONS AND GAAP-INSOLVENT
THRIFTS OBSERVED IN THE SUCCEEDING YEAR

Year	Number of Institutions Rated as Problems at Previous Year-End	Number of Resolutions and Remaining GAAP-Insolvencies
1981	159	167
1982	513	484
1983	720	363
1984	678	481
1985	738	534

Source: Tables 2-1 and 2-4.

react in timely fashion to easily observable information events that
indicated that FSLIC's risk exposure in the operations of these firms
was probably increasing rapidly. Perhaps the most obvious events
were the relatively high deposit interest rates being offered, and
various jumps and declines that could be observed in the stock prices
of zombie firms. It is important to recognize that most of the specific
strategic moves that could be made by an individual firm's management would almost certainly be covenanted and closely monitored
by a conscientious private guarantor. A partial list of potentially
ominous developments follows:

1) Decisions to emphasize new activities, such as originating acquisition, development, and construction loans for the purpose
   of selling participations in these loans to other firms. The riskiness of these strategies could be signalled by:
   —the formation of a mortgage corporation for out-of-state orig-
   inations as a subsidiary of the thrift's service corporation.
   (Such an event would emphasize that managers were moving
   outside their previous geographic and financial range of experience);
   —the extent to which borrower equity was lacking in the deals
   being made;
   —the height of the contract interest rates and fees being set on
   the loans made;
   —an increase in the proportion of the firm's net worth held in
   the form of goodwill. (The danger here is that, as an accounting entry that represents the amortized difference between
   the price paid to acquire a target firm and the appraised value
   of its separately identifiable assets and nonequity liabilities,

goodwill includes the capitalized value to the firm of FSLIC guarantees.)

2) Formation of an asset-liability committee whose charge was to emphasize deposit growth and not just to lessen interest-risk exposure. A number of related asset-liability developments also need to be examined for evidence of aggressive risk taking:

  —starting up extraregional or high profile Certificate of Deposit (CD) programs, which might indicate that managers were funding portfolio growth out of "hot money";

  —achieving unusually rapid deposit growth, which presumes higher than customary deposit rates (as mentioned earlier, high deposit rates themselves represent a classic signal of high risk activity);

  —surges or declines in the categorical composition of deposit accounts that go against industry patterns, suggesting that a thrift's incremental core business was not being built on customer convenience and service;

  —irregularities in project appraisal and review practices.

3) Filing of a plan to convert from a mutual to a stock association.

4) Establishment of a thrift holding company or rapid growth in the size of the thrift's service corporation.

5) Accumulating evidence that the firm's operations might be outgrowing management's capacity to manage the risks taken on:

  —sharp expansion in personnel;

  —extraordinary asset growth;

  —above-average growth in loan delinquencies;

  —sharp growth in reverse repurchase agreements;

  —sharp expansion in servicing fees;

  —industry scuttlebutt about conflicts of interest and irregular management practices.

THE EFFICIENCY OF MANAGERIAL TRADEOFFS BETWEEN RISK AND REWARD

Finance theory holds that the rate of return one can project for an efficient investment increases with the amount of risk undertaken. If guarantee charges are fixed, the risk to which a manager can prudently expose his or her firm's stockholders increases with the extent to which he or she believes the firm's debts are guaranteed by a credible outside party. Because of this credible outside guarantee, the firm can borrow funds at a relatively low rate of interest. If for the sake of argument we suppose that a FSLIC guarantee is almost as good as one from the U.S. Treasury, the firm could borrow at something approaching the yield on comparable Treasury debt. At the same time, the firm's projected return on capital would increase with the riskiness of its assets and business operations and fall with the amount of enterprise-contributed capital. The idea is that the riskier a guaranteed enterprise or its environment becomes, the greater the differential between what it can expect to earn on its funds and what it must pay its creditors (here, depositors) to support the project. Unless the guarantor imposes implicit or explicit charges that eliminate this differential, it is going to be victimized by at least some of its most venturesome and/or least capitalized clients.

Finance theory also establishes a criterion of investment "efficiency." An efficient portfolio is one that incorporates no uncompensated forms of risk bearing (i.e., none that can be costlessly diversified away) and that earns the market price for risk bearing for every risk it incorporates. As long as managers maintain an efficient portfolio, a decapitalized thrift's stockholders need not be damaged by highly speculative loans at the time loans are made. On the contrary, in the presence of FSLIC guarantees, a thrift's stock price could benefit greatly from such loans, given the reputed inadequacies in FSLIC's risk management system. Immediate stockholder damage would occur only if the firm's stockholders could not diversify away some of the diversifiable risks the firm assumed or if portfolio and business risks were not adequately compensated at the time the risks were taken.

A savings institution's management must risk the failure of the firm if it is to maximize its stockholders' benefits from deposit-insurance guarantees. Each individual stockholder could have diversified against underlying regional real estate or industrial risks or taken some or all of his share of the risky bets off the table at a profit by selling the firm's stock early in the game. Because thrifts are often closely held, substantial stock sales might in practice be hard to effect quickly at fair value. Nevertheless, manager-stockholders would have special reason to sell their stock if they knew that the firm's portfolio was inefficiently risky.

Distinguishing Go-For-Broke Financial Plays from Managerial Corruption and Negligence

To prove that a risk-taking manager failed to perform his or her economic duty to a firm's stockholders, it would be necessary to prove negligence or corruption. The negligence issue concerns: (1) the adequacy of staff procedures for risk analysis (i.e., methods for evaluating the borrower's character, balance sheet, income statements, and future economic projections) and (2) the avoidance of uncompensated risk. There is nothing necessarily fishy in a number of geographically or industrially concentrated real estate loans going sour at the same time. The same factors (e.g., a surprisingly long period of high interest rates or cumulative regional overbuilding) could ruin a number of a firm's borrowers or assets at the same time. For U.S. deposit institutions, such bunching is all the more likely because a lack of geographic and product-line diversification is inherent in the regional specialization imposed by branch-banking laws and in other forms of regulating the entry of deposit institutions into new activities and product markets.

Managerial corruption or negligence would be indicated if terms offered a thrift's borrowers were too soft relative to market prices or if potential receipts were unfairly diverted to managers' own use. For this reason, FSLIC examiners habitually investigate whether loan interest rates, fees, and contingent payments diverge from market norms.

Another control that helps to assure that the rewards anticipated in thrift lending and investments are at least proportionate to the risks is ongoing review of the firm's policies and decisions both by its board of directors and by outside accountants. Board members have a duty to understand the risks that develop in making loans to a limited number of borrowers. An outside board member has little value unless he or she has the capacity to decode what tend to be at least mildly self-serving managerial reports. Although danger signals are often buried in documentation, board members have a responsibility to make themselves understand the material management submits to them. Board involvement in overseeing loan decisions makes turnover in board members a potential sign of defective procedures and controls. Among the roles traditionally assigned to outside accountants is to identify corrupt or negligent decisions. If conscientious auditors were not disturbed by procedures and internal controls that a decapitalized thrift had in place when speculative investments were actually made, one may presume that procedures and controls seemed satisfactory to prudent outside observers.

Internal controls and procedures include project reviews by the Board's loan committee. What kind of criticism can reasonably be expected from a conscientious member of an institution's loan committee? In my experience as a member of a similar committee for a pension fund, loan proposals presented to a committee are usually framed in ways that dispose the committee to support the staff's analysis. This occurs partly because loan proposals that staff analysis screens out are not presented, although they may be summarized in some way. Raising tough or challenging questions in committee is in my experience as much as stockholders can expect from a prudent board member. A committee's staff does not like its analysis to be rejected and tends to deflect, rather than to confront the force of critical questions. Relative to staff, committee members work from an inherently disadvantageous knowledge base. Staff answers cannot be completely rejected as long as they maintain the ring of truth. But a committee member has the duty of making reasonably sure that the staff is honest, on its toes, and not missing any tricks in a proposed deal.

In evaluating the performance of a loan committee, it is important to recognize that differences in a property's appraisal values at different dates do not clearly establish an error in the earlier appraisal. Observed differences may trace to a change in local economic prospects. Similarly, later increases in loan-loss reserves do not imply the inadequacy of earlier appraisals. They may instead indicate the receipt of new information. To prove inadequate appraisals, FSLIC needs to show departures from trends in the changing value of comparable properties in applicable regions during the relevant time period.

A final question that examiners, accountants, and board members should review is whether managerial compensation seems unduly high. This requires a careful assessment of the risk premium that properly belongs in the salary of a manager who is presiding over a go-for-broke operation. Economic theory supports a need for zombie-firm stockholders to pay managers well for the hard-to-diversify riskiness to their careers that results from working for a firm whose stock value is being maximized by accepting a substantial risk of failure. For this reason, above-average salaries for thrift executives should serve as a signal for more detailed and more frequent examination.

Managerial Efficiency in FSLIC Liquidation and Nationalization Activities

Once FSLIC either takes over the management of a firm or undertakes to liquidate its assets, additional losses may develop from inefficiencies inherent in government operation. The problem is that the incentives that govern decisions in a government bureau typically depart substantially from those that are enforced in market-driven private enterprise.

In recent years, as FSLIC acquired thousands of properties across the nation, Congress and OMB refused to give FSLIC officials either the staff or the funds to manage acquired assets appropriately. Far from accepting blame for this, since mid-1987 congressional oversight committees have held hearings to go on record as critics of important elements of FSLIC's liquidation and deal-making performance. After FSLIC stepped up its rate of insolvency resolution in the last half of 1988, the scapegoating became particularly intense.

FDIC Chairman Seidman has repeatedly emphasized that a government insurer causes an asset's value to decline when it takes control of it. Limiting this loss of value was one of the arguments for establishing a special asset disposition corporation for FSLIC in the mid-1980s. However, the resulting entity (the Federal Asset Disposition Association) performed poorly and is slated for phaseout.

When FSLIC is fully bailed out, part of the bill presented to taxpayers will be for the FDIC-FSLIC management team's inefficiencies as liquidators. To increase accountability, taxpayers must demand current documentation that FSLIC and FDIC bureaucrats are not selling the assets of failed or failing firms on disadvantageous terms. To put the issue into broader perspective, Congress ought to require FSLIC and the FDIC to produce evidence on how well they have performed on average as receivers in the past and to establish procedures for providing full and timely analysis of their performance in the future.

SUMMARY AND TRANSITION

This chapter defines the role played by a firm's capital and describes the character of FSLIC's policies for regulating client capital positions in recent years. The analysis seeks to explain why decapitalized FSLIC clients would be attracted to strategies of aggressive growth and risk taking. Understanding how a firm's incentives change as its capital declines shows that it is wrong to presume without additional evidence that the FSLIC-insured thrifts that eventually recorded mammoth losses were ineptly or corruptly managed.

Chapter three explores the question of what FSLIC officials should have known and should have done about the unbooked losses being imposed on FSLIC during the 1970s and 1980s by client risk taking, particularly at economically insolvent firms. We identify three critical mistakes in FSLIC policy. To supply perspective on the reasons for these mistakes, we introduce the concepts of principal-agent conflicts and incentive-incompatible contracts.

Notes

1. During the 1980s, home builders bought many now-troubled S&Ls and may be seen to have played a prominent role in the insolvency of Texas thrifts.

2. Professional accounting guidelines dictating the reclassification of low-equity commercial real estate loans were first issued by the American Institute of Certified Public Accountants on November 30, 1983 and were not adopted by the FHLBB until much later.

References

American Banker. 1988. "Ranking the Financial PACs: Who Are the Big Fundraisers?" (June 27), p. 11.

Barth, James R., and Michael G. Bradley. 1988. "Thrift Deregulation and Federal Deposit Insurance." Washington: Office of Policy and Economic Research, Federal Home Loan Bank Board. Paper prepared for Perspectives on Banking Regulation Conference, Federal Reserve Bank of Cleveland (November).

Jackson, Brooks. 1989. "As Thrift Industry's Troubles and Losses Mounted, its PACs' Donations to Key Congressmen Surged." *Wall Street Journal* (February 7), p. A26.

Kane, Edward J. 1981. "Reregulation, Savings and Loan Diversification, and the Flow of Housing Finance," in *Savings and Loan Asset Management under Deregulation.* San Francisco: Federal Home Loan Bank of San Francisco, pp. 81–109.

_____. 1982. "S&Ls and Interest-Rate Reregulation: The FSLIC as an In-Place Bailout Program." *Housing Finance Review* 1 (July), pp. 219–243.

Stern, Philip M., 1988. *The Best Congress Money Can Buy.* New York: Pantheon Books.

Strunk, Norman, and Fred Case. 1988. *Where Deregulation Went Wrong: A Look at the Causes Behind Savings and Loan Failures in the 1980s.* Washington: U.S. League of Savings Institutions.

Chapter Three

IDENTIFYING AND UNDERSTANDING
FSLIC'S CRITICAL MISTAKES

It is instructive to divide the operations of any corporation into activities of production, financing, and marketing. When deposit insurance is provided by a government entity, marketing and financing activities are more subtle than they may appear at first glance. I defer these subtleties to the next chapter where FSLIC is analyzed as if it were a corporation with a stock value that depends on managerial decisions of many kinds.

In this chapter, a deposit insurer's principal activities are reduced to two functions that FSLIC handled particularly poorly: reserving for and managing its net exposure to risk. The mistakes FSLIC made in these two activities reinforced each other. Under-reserving for its implicit losses made its lapses in risk management seem less consequential.

Active risk management is required because a fundamental asymmetry exists between the claims that a client institution and its insurer have to unanticipated profits and losses that the institution may accumulate. A deposit insurer manages its risk exposure by monitoring and controlling the potential losses to which the activities of client financial institutions expose its reserves. Data are presented to show that FSLIC was short of reserves for many years and that information and techniques by which to ascertain this fact were available to FSLIC officials.

INNOCENT VERSUS GUILTY MISTAKES

As emphasized in chapter two, financial institutions are engaged in an inherently risky business. In either directly investing in a risky project or indirectly guaranteeing it, what an institution does not or cannot know is what stands to generate losses. An investor's wealth is exposed to two sources of risk from lack of information. The first comes from information the investor does not know that is in principle knowable at the time the investment is made. Some of this information might in fact be known by some of the parties involved in financing or carrying out the project. The second kind of risk comes from information that cannot be known until the project begins to play itself out.

The first type of risk can be reduced or eliminated by careful research and analysis. The second cannot. For example, by asking questions or reading the newspapers carefully, a bettor may be able to ascertain that a football team's star player is not going to be able to play in a key game. However, no one can know in advance how well or how poorly the remainder of the team or its opponents will actually play on gameday.

In assessing an unsuccessful enterprise, this distinction clarifies why the practice of Monday morning quarterbacking is often an unfair one. It is only fair is to criticize people for using knowable information incorrectly or for not bothering to acquire such information when it would have been economic to acquire it. In assessing the FSLIC's decline, fairness dictates that we explore three main questions:

(1) Who knew or should have known important "knowable" information?

(2) When did they either know or become obligated to know this information?

(3) What should they have done to represent politicians' or taxpayers' best interests when this information came into their possession?

Studying how and why an industry and its supporting government insurer have gone wrong is an exercise in pathology. A pathologist has two major objectives: learning how to avoid a replay of the problem in the future, and assigning blame. In researching the first issue, the focus is a constructive one: to isolate a set of either workable or ideal reforms that have the potential to have either prevented or greatly ameliorated the painful outcome we are experiencing. In investigating the second issue, the focus tends to degenerate into a destructive one: analysis tends to undermine the reputations of particular parties who might have avoided or lessened the problem by acting more energetically or insightfully (but did not do so).

Although it is not this book's principal purpose to parcel out blame, blame must nevertheless be assessed and assigned. But the reader should not mistake my blame analysis for a personal attack on individual regulators and politicians. Such scolding degenerates into mean-spirited scapegoating that would distract attention from institutional and incentive reforms that are in this case badly needed. Everyone makes mistakes. It is ordinarily easier to forgive ourselves and others for mistakes once we understand why they occurred. In deposit insurance, we need to put right the framework within which past mistakes occurred as soon and as fully as possible.

To establish the extent of my sympathy for individual regulators, I want to begin by recounting a perspective-setting true story. In 1966, I left a three-year-old son in the back seat of my car while I stepped out to talk with a friend. Naturally, I put the car in park, shut off the ignition, and took the keys with me.

While my friend and I were talking, my car began to roll down the grade on which I had parked it. I was horrified to see the gleeful satisfaction that my son had taken in moving himself into the driver's seat. His glee turned to acute distress when the car smashed into my friend's vehicle, which as it turned out stood only about 12 feet down the hill.

Naturally, I rushed over to make sure that my son was all right. When I reached him, he was so distraught that he could only say one thing. He kept screaming over and over, "How did that *happen?*"

As I tried to comfort him, I realized that his question could be interpreted in two distinct ways: in terms of the physical causes of the event or in terms of where to place the blame. Moreover, the answer to the first question—that *he* had disengaged the park lever and allowed gravity to take over—gave a very misleading view of where the blame lay.

The moral responsibility for this event was almost exclusively mine. I had on several occasions allowed my son to play with the car's steering wheel in the driveway to our home. Because the park lever was always engaged and our driveway was absolutely flat, this seemed completely safe. I had failed both to emphasize to him sufficiently that in any other context it was unwise to treat a car as a plaything or to recognize that my son might learn merely by watching me that disengaging the car from park was among the first things a "real" driver did.

I see important parallels between the parental myopia and tunnel vision that set up my son's minicrash and the regulatory thinking and behavior that set up the economic ruin of FSLIC. Two principal and (I believe) readily forgivable common features are: (1) a failure to anticipate the dangers of a *major shift in the environment* for

FSLIC in the volatility of prices, in the rate of technological change, and in the degree of client insolvency—one that rendered preexisting risk-management policies inadequate; and (2) a failure to anticipate the *strength of the incentives* that children/regulatees had to move out of safe "back seat" positions into aggressive "front seat" ones.

However, when a dose of harsh reality educated us on these scores, politicians and FSLIC officials responded very differently than I did. While I took every reasonable action I could think of both to re-motivate my son and to keep him away from the wheel in the future, FSLIC officials (acting under constraints imposed by the politicians to whom they report) adopted a strategy of denying the problem, suppressing critical information, granting regulatory forbearances, and extending expanded powers to troubled clients. They gambled on the possibility that time alone would cure the problem. They hoped that, with access to new powers and more funding, most of their decapitalized regulatees could and would simply grow out the problem.

From the point of view of society, this gamble was a bad one. This miscalculation is the most serious and least defensible failure of the three: equivalent to taking a third strike in baseball. This chapter and the next seek to explain why politicians or regulators may be expected to deal with parallel problems less firmly than a typical parent would. The difference lies in the possibility of conflicts between regulators' and politicians' reputations and career interests and the public good.

LAYERING OF INCENTIVE INCOMPATIBILITY

To explain these conflicts, economists have developed a number of specialized concepts and distinctions, some of which have painfully jargonistic names. The most fundamental are the concepts of *incentives* and *incentive-incompatible contracts*. Every decision takes place against a background of economic and noneconomic incentives, each of which (like a muledriver's use of carrots and sticks) pushes and pulls the decisionmaker toward or away from alternative courses of action. Essentially, an *incentive* (or counterincentive) is a foreseeable benefit (or cost) that leads a decisionmaker to find one set of actions more desirable than another. Contractual arrangements are called *incentive-incompatible* when provisions lead some of the parties to a financial contract to work to the disadvantage of other contracting parties.

In the United States today, federal deposit insurance (whether it is administered by the FDIC or FSLIC) is an incentive-incompatible scheme. This scheme has the unfortunate feature that the degree of incompatibility between the contracting parties (depositors, insured institutions, regulators, politicians, and taxpayers) increases as an insured institution's stockholder-contributed (or mutual) capital declines. A decapitalized institution faces enormous incentives to undertake go-for-broke financial plays that load potential losses onto uninformed and insufficiently wary taxpayers, while depositors, regulators, and politicians have some incentive to look the other way. FSLIC's failure to counter these incentives and its habitual delay in recognizing and disciplining innovative forms of risk taking at solvent and insolvent clients alike are rooted in incentive breakdowns between them and taxpayers. FSLIC officials face political and economic pressures that lead them to behave in ways that diverge importantly from the long-run interest of the taxpayers who ultimately underwrite FSLIC's operations. A layered breakdown in incentives—between FSLIC and its clients, between elected politicians and FSLIC, and between politicians and taxpayers—has turned a horde of zombie deposit institutions loose upon our land.

Relationships between taxpayers and politicians, between politicians and government regulators, and even between deposit insurers and their clients may usefully be conceived as examples of a *principal-agent relationship*. In any such relationship, one party (the principal) may be viewed as implicitly or explicitly contracting with the second party (the agent) to perform a set of tasks for the principal. The economic relationship is one of explicit or implicit delegation. The basis of the relationship is to leverage the time, skills, or information base of the principal by shifting the responsibility for performing a class of activities to the agent.

Ideally, every principal would like its agents to perform the delegated activities exactly as the principal would choose to do them if the principal had the time, talent, or information available to the agents. What makes principal-agent relationships an important field of study is the real-world difficulty of establishing a completely incentive-compatible relationship. Typically, an agent faces temptations to promote its own welfare at the expense of that of the principal. Portraying this idea in an exaggerated fashion, an Eastern European saying holds that a mouse is safer in the mouth of a cat than is a widow's estate in the hands of a lawyer.

A considerable body of contemporary research in finance is directed to the issue of how financial instruments and institutions

effectively bond and monitor the behavior of agents to limit opportunities for them to engage in exploitively self-serving behavior (e.g.,
Jensen and Meckling 1975). In attempting to apply these concepts
to decision making in government, an important complication arises,
because the interests of various individual citizens or taxpayers often
diverge substantially (Wagner 1986). The concept of principal becomes very abstract, and the interest of taxpayers as a whole must
be viewed as a hypothetical consensus of some kind. This consensus
presumes the existence of a weighting process that allows for distributional conflict and external effects which occur when the actions
of one set of citizens impose uncompensated costs or benefits on one
or more other citizens.

With this proviso, we may define agency costs as welfare or resource losses that result from conflicts between the interests of taxpayer principals and the specific interests of government bureaus
and officials that political processes designate to serve as their agents.
Agency costs have two components: (1) the explicit costs of monitoring, bonding, and other arrangements to lessen principal-agent
conflicts and (2) losses that are incurred implicitly because residual
elements of conflict are left unresolved by the conflict-controlling
arrangements society has established.

Recognizing political pressures generated by distributional conflict and external effects as well as the existence of principal-agent
problems helps to explain the occurrence of what appear from an
economic perspective to be regulatory mistakes. Resulting incentive
problems tempt officials to defer needed regulatory adjustments and
to suppress unfavorable information about the consequences of these
and other short-sighted regulatory decisions.

It is doubtful that politicians and regulators see themselves as
behaving myopically in ways that victimize taxpayers. For this reason, some of the players whose decisions worsened the FSLIC mess
will treat the criticism offered here as uninformed accusation. Their
main point will be that they *know* what was in their minds when
various coverup and forbearance decisions were made and it was
surely *not* exploiting taxpayers. But this objection misses the heart
of my case. Decisionmakers are often imperfectly aware of the true
motives that underlie the choices they make. Incentives can make
themselves felt through unconscious and subconscious implicit calculations just as effectively as through an explicit and conscious
sorting out of costs and benefits. Decisionmakers routinely process
a complex flow of informational signals that arrive simultaneously
from labor and financial markets, colleagues, supervisors and clients,

and from their individual consciences. In his or her everyday life, everyone formulates strategic responses to such conflicting signals almost reflexively.

Officials' claims to have been blindsided by the expanding costs of deposit-insurance subsidies to risk taking testify to an *insensitivity* to their need to analyze the *long-run consequences* of the policies they follow. What is most disturbing about this insensitivity is that it suggests a systematic anesthetization of official consciences to the moral dimensions of the tradeoffs being made under the impetus of political pressure. In choosing not to reserve explicitly for appraisable losses that were plainly developing in decapitalized clients, FSLIC officials strengthened the industry's credibility before Congress and therefore its capacity to lobby against more effective regulation. Not reporting loss appraisals meant that client losses had to make themselves felt in official accounting records before regulators could begin to bring them under control.

Listening to regulators' and politicians' defense of these ultimately indefensible actions leads me to conclude that the modern code of public service has three unspoken precepts. First, almost anything may be okay if one can keep from getting caught at it. Second, even if caught, one's behavior may still be okay if one can find a credible scapegoat on which to pin the blame. Third, even when scapegoating fails, one may still be exonerated by claiming that there was nothing else that one could reasonably do.

Milton tells us that the third justification—necessity—is an easily abused rationale:

So spake the Fiend, and with necessity,
the tyrant's plea, excus'd his devilish deeds.

(*Paradise Lost*, Book IV, l. 393)

What makes necessity a lame excuse is the implicit claim that, for society, the actions chosen were better than all other options. Among the options that ought to have been considered are many personally painful and dangerous ones. Chief among these would be trying to overcome congressional resistance by using one's official position as a "bully pulpit." A top official could develop persuasive data with which to alert the press and therefore the taxpayer as to the extent and dangers of capital forbearance, and plan to resign pointedly if Congress refuses to come around. If evidence developed that Congress chose to believe old friends and supporters within the thrift industry over its top regulatory officials, a conscientious regulator should find this to be an intolerable situation. In rejecting this personally risky strategy for the option of being a good soldier, a public servant effectively gambles on his or her ability either to overcome the odds by dint of extraordinary developments or to effect a clean getaway before the long-run consequences of the failed gamble can emerge.

FSLIC's basic mistakes were: (1) to remain sanguine for two decades about interest-induced declines in the market value of their clients' capital; (2) to provide decapitalized firms in a troubled industry explicit regulatory relief, both in the amount of capital required and, still worse, in how capital was measured for regulatory purposes; and (3) to permit economically decapitalized clients to pursue *new and old* forms of risk taking without imposing appropriate safeguards against the pursuit of speculative projects that impose losses on FSLIC. Regulators' slowness to appreciate how rapidly and how extensively new instruments and new activities were burdening FSLIC reserves served to compound these basic mistakes.

Like insects, zombie thrifts developed in two principal stages. Their "larva" stage occurred when increases in interest rates brought on by accelerating inflation and subsequent disinflation policies wiped out the market value of the capital of much of the thrift industry. Most zombies completed their transition into mature pests when, instead of requiring troubled firms to recapitalize or else, federal officials helped decapitalized firms cover up their weakness and thereby conceal parallel weaknesses in FSLIC reserves. This coverup permitted a great number of decapitalized firms to operate without stockholder-contributed or mutual capital (which we term enterprise-contributed net worth) in an environment that was rich in opportunities to make and lose funds in a hurry.

These policies of covering up and not explicitly financing (i.e., reserving for FSLIC's implicit losses) represent an unhealthy or negative-present-value type of "gambling" by politicians and regulators. This chapter documents the major effects of the kinds of gambles that federal officials have made, and explains officials' disposition to making socially perverse gambles as behavior that is rational precisely because of principal-agent conflicts.

TURNING A BLIND EYE TO THE UNBOOKED INTEREST-INDUCED DECAPITALIZATION OF THRIFT INSTITUTIONS[1]

Some opinionmakers incorrectly attribute the thrift industry's current predicament to two major changes in their federal regulatory environment: (1) the phased removal of deposit-rate ceilings that was mandated by the Depository Institutions Deregulation and Monetary Control Act of 1980 (DIDMCA), and (2) legislative decisions to expand thrifts' range of permissible loan and investment opportunities. This diagnosis of the problem suggests that reintroducing ceilings on explicit deposit rates and paring back the list of permissible thrift activities could be relied upon to prevent a replay of the current thrift crisis. This view is dangerously simplistic and embodies two important mistakes.

First, the benefits that depository institutions reaped from federal ceilings on their explicit deposit rates had been eroding from the moment they were first extended to thrifts in late 1966. The problem is that, whenever interest rates on comparable securities rise above ceiling rates on deposits, knowledgeable customers have an incentive to look for other places to put their funds and for ways to extract additional implicit interest from their depository. This shifts the focus of competition among institutions subject to the ceilings from explicit interest to implicit interest and to the development of deposit substitutes. Many ways to pay implicit interest were in fact used, including: merchandise premiums; finders fees; free or subsidized expansions in available customer services; and an accelerated spread of branch offices and off-premises automated teller machines. In fact, during the era of deposit-rate ceilings, particularly wily customers were able to extract enough implicit interest to saddle above-market funding costs on their deposit institution. Deposit substitutes developed by depository institutions to pay market levels of explicit interest included retail repurchase agreements and asset-participation arrangements. Particularly damaging to thrifts were deposit substitutes developed by securities firms: money-market mutual funds and cash-management accounts which exploited ongoing technological advances in computer record keeping and telecommunications. Between 1971 and early 1980, the funds placed in such instruments grew from about $1 billion to about $230 billion. Hence, irrespective of the disputed regulatory actions taken in the early 1980s, technological and competitive forces were already steadily squeezing the profit margins of savings institutions.

Second, thrifts' narrow pre-1980 charters did not stop them from making ruinous longshot bets when they became economically insolvent. When thrift institutions' assets and liabilities are appraised and accounted at market values, it becomes obvious that the fact of widespread industry insolvency predated the policy measures of the early 1980s. Far from being the root cause of industry losses, the

1980 and 1982 policy adjustments were conceived as a response to unbooked but appraisable losses already imbedded in the industry's large overhang of low-rate mortgage loans. Twenty years' worth of official commissions and study groups asked to investigate the need for financial reform had recommended jettisoning deposit-rate ceilings and giving thrift institutions broader investment powers. Along with the expansion in deposit-insurance coverage from $40,000 to $100,000 per account, the policy adjustments were seen as ways of increasing the economic value of thrift franchises by permitting thrifts simultaneously to expand their deposit base and to invest the funds they raised on a more diversified basis.

This analysis does not deny that legislators and regulators made policy mistakes in 1980 and 1982. It merely says that deposit-rate deregulation was not one of them, and that expanding thrifts' asset powers created problems primarily because federal deposit insurance was allowed to remain mispriced and misadministered. To repeat, the fatal elements of misadministration consisted of:

☐ pooh-poohing the unbooked but easily appraisable losses imbedded in thrift portfolios;
☐ helping economically insolvent institutions to live with their insolvency; and
☐ resisting economists' attempts to educate elected officials as to how severely a condition of unbooked economic insolvency distorts risk-taking incentives at insured firms.

Interest Rate Risk: Roots and Consequences

Recurrent thrift-institution crises arise from these firms' seeming addiction to taking substantial portfolio risks. The industry's balance sheet is risky in two ways. First, it is highly levered. This means that the value of assets held is a high multiple of industry net worth. Second, the average savings institution finances itself with liabilities that are, on balance, much shorter in their average life than the assets it holds. This practice is called "short-funding." This term serves to emphasize that such a financing strategy creates a gap between the average lives of the future cash flows generated, respectively, on the asset side and on the liability side of an institution's balance sheet.

Short-funding implies a risky mismatching of the lives of an institution's assets and liabilities. On average, the liabilities of thrifts turn over much faster than their assets do. This exposes their incomes and capital to loss from interest increases and from interest volatility.

On the one hand, unanticipated increases in interest rates narrow spreads between accounting yields attributable to the assets already on their books and the institution's overall cost of funds. On the other hand, although unanticipated decreases in interest rates widen these spreads, they also encourage borrowers to prepay and refinance their debt. The wider the swings that occur in interest rates, the greater the chance that at some point enterprise-contributed capital can become exhausted.

It is a mistake to believe that a mortgage-lending orientation in itself forces a thrift institution's managers to operate with a mismatched asset and liability position. An institution that originates long-term loans can control the gap between the average life of its asset and liability positions in at least four complementary ways: issue more long-term liabilities; stress variable interest rate or shorter-maturity loans; package the loans it originates for resale in secondary markets; or hedge its net exposure to interest-volatility risk by transactions in some combination of interest rate futures contracts, forward contracts, or options contracts. However, although mortgage resales and variable rate lending increased dramatically in the 1980s, few thrifts can be said to have held hedged positions in recent years. Jumps in interest rates and in interest rate volatility—such as those associated with the Federal Reserve's well-publicized efforts from October 1979 to mid-1982 to break the back of inflation by holding down the monetary growth rate—cause immediate economic losses to short-funded institutions. Moreover, the less capital a firm has when such jumps begin, the quicker the adapting interest rate environment can run through the value of its enterprise-contributed net worth.

Until the 1970s, thrift institutions' predominant financing vehicle was the passbook savings account. But competitive pressures generated by the interaction of accelerating inflation with unrealistically low ceilings on passbook interest rates encouraged the proliferation of higher rate forms of savings certificates and the development of negotiable order of withdrawal (NOW) accounts. Along with expanded opportunities for advantageous S&L borrowing from the Federal Home Loan Bank System, by the 1980s this process had remade the liability side of thrift balance sheets. Because thrift institutions are highly levered and in most cases continue to hold assets whose average life substantially exceeds the average life of even these reconstituted liabilities, unanticipated run-ups in interest rates (such as occurred in the 34 months that ended in July 1982) place the industry in a precarious condition.

As interest rates and servicing costs on deposits soared above the contract yields on outstanding thrift assets, newspaper articles on thrift institutions turned unfavorable. Projecting various firms' negative accounting earnings into the indefinite future, some analysts morbidly began to count down the months of life expectancy left to them. They did this without realizing that the low contract rates on thrift assets had already rendered the firms on their watch list insolvent on a properly capitalized basis.

Confused by the inadequacies of historical-cost accounting, reporters depicted firms in the thrift industry as though fate had involuntarily enrolled them in a financial dance marathon, a contest in which they were expected to keep dancing until their individual resources were exhausted. The level of interest rates was seen as setting the tempo at which the contest orchestra played. The faster the beat and the longer an up-tempo rhythm was maintained, the more rapidly the market value of the bookable net worth of individual thrift institutions would be used up. The dance-marathon perspective severely misrepresents both what an institution's resources actually were *and* when its capital was damaged by surges in interest rates and interest rate volatility. It portrays the problem as if it lies in the delayed impact of below-market future accounting earnings on the future value of accounting net worth, rather than in the immediate decline that rising interest rates cause in the market value of a short-funded institution's capital position. The immediate impact of interest-induced asset revaluations on the market value of a short-funded institution's assets is greater than their impact on the institution's value of deposit and nondeposit debt. Treating this revaluation as occurring slowly over time overstates the interim accounting value of enterprise-contributed net worth, and understates the value of FSLIC's explicit and implicit guarantees of each client's deposit debt.

Holdings of low-interest mortgage instruments were an obvious source of weakness in S&L and savings bank balance sheets. Far less obvious was the way that FSLIC's partial suspensions of effective capital requirements increased the value of its guarantees of economically insolvent thrift institutions' deposits. Across the universe of the honestly run thrifts that authorities proved consistently loath to close, the value of deposit-insurance guarantees largely offset unbooked losses on S&L and savings-bank mortgages. But the economic consequences of this policy were not explained to federal taxpayers: that responsibility for these mortgage losses had been passed through

to FSLIC and to the unknown taxpayers who constitute this government-sponsored corporation's ultimate guarantors.

**The Size of the Pre-Deregulation Interest-Induced Decapitalization of
FSLIC-Insured Institutions**

Rough measures of the impact of unbooked interest-induced losses
on thrift industry losses have been constructed on an appraisal bases
for 1971–83 by Kane (1985) and with somewhat greater precision
for 1980–84 by Brumbaugh (1988). Table 3-1 reports the ratio of what
we may call market-value net worth to total assets at FSLIC thrifts,
between 1971 and 1984. To correct in a conservative way for an
acknowledged upward bias in Kane's method, his figures are reduced
by one-third to produce a time series whose order of magnitude
promises to be reliable over time.

These figures clarify that thrifts have been in crisis since at least
1971 and that the industry's shortage of enterprise-contributed capital was particularly severe during 1979–82. Although the 1983 and
1984 calculations show a distinct improvement in industry capital-

Table 3-1 ESTIMATES OF THE RATIO OF MARKET-VALUE NET
WORTH TO TOTAL ASSETS AT FSLIC-INSURED THRIFTS,
1971–84 (percent)

Year	Unadjusted Kane Estimates	Kane Estimates Reduced by One-Third	Brumbaugh Estimates
1971	− 5.66	− 3.77	---
1972	− 8.15	− 5.43	---
1973	− 6.96	− 4.64	---
1974	− 11.32	− 7.55	---
1975	− 11.66	− 7.77	---
1976	− 10.87	− 7.25	---
1977	− 9.93	− 6.62	---
1978	− 10.31	− 6.87	---
1979	− 13.99	− 9.32	---
1980	− 19.17	− 12.78	− 12.47
1981	− 23.12	− 15.41	− 17.32
1982	− 15.94	− 10.63	− 12.03
1983	− 9.05	− 6.03	− 5.64
1984	---	---	− 2.74

Sources: Kane (1985), p. 102, and Brumbaugh (1988), p. 50.

ization, circumstances make these calculations less relevant for the post-1982 era than they were before. The principal circumstance is that these market-value measurements focus on only one source of market-value fluctuation: that due to changes in interest rates. As the thrift business grew more complex after 1980 and especially after 1982, the risks that impacted the market value of their assets and liabilities became more complex too. A second problem is that these calculations conceal some of the negative value of the capital that needs to be recorded for zombie thrifts by offsetting it against the positive values recorded by their healthy competitors. These points come together in that many of the deeply insolvent thrifts, whose interest-induced 1979–82 losses had been neglected, used the respite provided by post-1982 FSLIC capital forbearance to load up with other kinds of longshot risks. At about three-fourths of these thrifts, the post-1982 interest-induced capital gains on their mortgage port-folios were not sufficient to offset losses incurred on speculative (and in some cases downright fraudulent) loans and investments.

TWO WAYS TO RESERVE FOR THE ASSET-QUALITY PROBLEMS DEVELOPING AFTER 1982

During the 1970s and very early 1980s, it is relatively easy to cal-culate on an industry basis, at least to a first approximation, fluc-tuations in the market value of mortgage loans. This is because these fluctuations were driven by nationwide swings in market interest rates rather than changes in the default risk on particular classes of loans. From 1983 on, imbedded losses in troubled thrifts have been driven far more by collapsing prospects for individual investments, loans, and loan collateral than by nationwide movements in interest rates. Because the depth of asset-quality problems varies regionally and with the industrial composition of an institution's obligors, es-timates of the impact of post-1982 asset-quality problems must be constructed in less aggregate ways. This section focuses on making use of the knowledge that some accounting approaches do a much better job than others of indicating that an individual institution's enterprise-contributed capital is under water.

FSLIC's current shortage of explicit capital centers around losses to it that are imbedded in the operations of zombie firms. A sensible way to estimate these losses is to construct and analyze a series of alternative estimates of the capital positions of institutions that fall in the zombie category.

While the economic insolvency of the worst zombies is likely to be identified by any reasonable method of accounting, troubled entities can use valuation options provided by historical-cost GAAP to structure their accounts to conceal some of their capital shortfall. These principles focus primarily on cataloguing resources that are tangible in nature and on registering obligations, expenditures, and receipts that occur in explicit and verifiable transactions.

Additional options to book intangible and implicit values were created by the deceptively asymmetric regulatory accounting principles (RAP) FSLIC adopted in 1982. Compared to GAAP, RAP accounting may exaggerate an institution's capital by weighting goodwill more generously than GAAP and by asymmetrically deferring unrealized losses but permitting unrealized gains to be booked immediately.

RAP's valuation options permit GAAP-insolvent thrifts to meet FSLIC capital requirements artificially. Managers of failing firms have strong incentives to mask their firms' insolvency. We must expect them to uncover and exploit options inherent in the GAAP and RAP accounting systems to generate an overly optimistic accounting assessment of an economically insolvent firm's capital position.

To strip away some of the potentially questionable sources of value that RAP and GAAP accounting allow S&Ls to put on their balance sheets, Veribanc, Inc. (located in Woburn, Mass.) has been tracking the number of S&Ls that show earning problems or that are insolvent on two stricter sets of principles. Veribanc calls the concepts of capital featured in its less forgiving measurement systems "GAAP-like net worth" and "tangible net worth," respectively. Veribanc's estimates of an intermediate concept we may loosely call "regulatory GAAP" are built up from reports of a firm's RAP net worth by disallowing completely such potentially questionable RAP-recognized values as: Garn-St Germain capital measurement innovations such as net worth certificates and qualifying subordinated debentures; "appraised equity capital" (whose weakness lies not in recognizing the appraised value of unrealized capital gains, but in asymmetrically ignoring the appraised value of unrealized capital losses); and deferred losses on loans and other assets sold. GAAP-like capital is obtained by eliminating goodwill and other intangible assets from regulatory GAAP. To obtain *tangible net worth*, GAAP-like capital is reduced by a "loan portfolio discount adjustment" designed to discount a firm's portfolio of loans and leases for the extent to which it is underperforming the industry average. The loan portfolio discount adjustment parallels the methods used by Kane and Brumbaugh to discount thrift mortgage holdings during 1971–84. Using loss rates and a measure of pre-Garn-St Germain GAAP capital, Veribanc compiles a watch list of troubled firms that it classifies into a so-called "red category."

For the 18 quarters running from 1984.2 to 1988.3, table 3-2 lists the number of thrifts categorized as showing each of four economic problems: (1) an operating loss in the current quarter; (2) a loss rate sufficient to exhaust net worth within one year; (3) classification in Veribanc's Red category; and (4) a negative tangible net worth. Trends in the number of firms falling in each category deliver a mixture of good and bad news. The good news is that over these 18 quarters the number of "red" institutions declines by 35 percent and the number with negative tangible net worth declines by 42 percent. The bad news is that the number operating at a loss each quarter remains high (over 25 percent of the industry) and the number whose loss rate is sufficient to exhaust net worth within a year (though coming down from its peak in 1987.4) rises to twice its 1984.2 value.

These data support the view that capital forbearance—which has to an important extent been forced on FSLIC by Congress, both in its unwillingness to increase FSLIC's human or capital resources to handle the surge in client economic insolvencies and in formal limitations on closure powers enacted in the Competitive Equality Banking Act of 1987—served to bifurcate the industry into the living and the living dead. While many of the living have been able to strengthen their capital position, the zombies have been getting worse.

The growth of imbedded losses at S&Ls that were insolvent on each of Veribanc's three bases is shown for 1987–88 in table 3-3. Until the third quarter of 1988 (when FSLIC was sharply stepping up its rate of insolvency resolution) and within each insolvency category, losses, capital, and owned real estate deteriorated virtually quarter by quarter. This deterioration strongly supports the argument that capital forbearance has been costly and wrong-headed both for FSLIC and for the federal taxpayers who must ultimately make good on its bills.

A Procedure for Calculating FSLIC's Loss Exposure in Insolvent Institutions Only

A ballpark estimate of the 1987.1 to 1988.3 evolution of the accumulating loss to FSLIC imbedded in the operations of GAAP-like insolvent and tangible-insolvent firms is shown in table 3-4. The estimate is constructed in three steps. First, it takes 100 percent of the deficiency in tangible net worth at GAAP-like insolvent S&Ls.

Then, it adds to this 75 percent of the *additional* deficiency at tangible-insolvent S&Ls. Finally, it deducts an allowance for losses in repossessed collateral equal to 50 percent of the value of real estate owned by tangible-insolvent S&Ls.

The weights used are chosen arbitrarily. In particular, applying a zero weight to intangible assets is very severe; some intangible assets may at some firms represent meaningful sources of value. Scaling down the weights used would, of course, lessen our estimate of FSLIC's unrecognized losses in tangible-insolvent S&Ls. However, on the other side of the coin, the calculation neglects a number of potentially important other sources of loss to FSLIC.

First, it makes no allowance either for FSLIC's liquidation costs or for other costs it incurs in unwinding an insolvent firm's affairs. Second, the loan-portfolio discount adjustment incorporated in tangible net worth may fail to correct completely for assets whose book values exceed their market worth. Far more importantly, the measure produced here makes no effort to calculate losses to FSLIC likely to be imbedded in near-insolvent S&Ls or to reserve for the risk of further net losses posed across the universe of firms whose deposits it guarantees. Observers judge many of FSLIC's recent insolvency resolutions to be so thinly capitalized as to deserve the name "boomerang financings." This means that because they impose substantial obligations on FSLIC to make good whatever losses finally develop, they have a good chance of returning to haunt the agency at a later date.

According to the order-of-magnitude evidence compiled in table 3-4, FSLIC has been losing on average more than $1 billion *per month* in the operation of insolvent or zombie S&Ls. The policy of forbearance that has produced these escalating losses is a public policy disgrace for which there is much blame to go around.

A More General Loss-Calculation Procedure

A more general way to estimate FSLIC's imbedded losses in any class of client institutions is to partition client institutions into different risk classes and to model FSLIC's appraised losses in each class as the product of three factors:

1. The amount of assets held in the given class of institution.
2. The percentage of the class's assets expected to require FSLIC-assisted insolvency resolution.
3. The cost per dollar of assets of resolving client insolvencies at institutions in this class.

Table 3-2 NUMBER OF THRIFTS THAT VERIBANC, INC., DETERMINED TO BE SUFFERING FROM VARIOUS UNFAVORABLE CONDITIONS, 1984–88, BY QUARTER

Quarter	Operated at a Loss during the Quarter	Loss Rate Sufficient to Exhaust Net Worth within One Year	Classified in Veribanc's Red Category	Tangible Net Worth is Negative	Total Number of Thrifts Reporting
1984.2	768	209	1,063	1,271	3,172
1984.3	966	238	1,065	1,420	3,161
1984.4	881	250	1,073	1,393	3,160
1985.1	910	256	1,259	1,370	3,186
1985.2	549	208	966	1,347	3,207
1985.3	613	235	928	1,254	3,252
1985.4	679	272	872	1,179	3,273
1986.1	602	284	818	1,104	3,280
1986.2	678	307	799	1,100	3,276

1986.3	746	337	782	972	3,264
1986.4	836	365	769	960	3,254
1987.1	690	361	724	960	3,238
1987.2	1,061	438	746	1,000	3,225
1987.3	935	452	765	963	3,213
1987.4	1,068	491	764	985	3,172
1988.1	955	467	757	931	3,141
1988.2	910	467	743	930	3,113
1988.3	837	419	691	735	3,046

Source: Veribanc's "Summary of Key S&L Problem Indicators over the Past Year," distributed privately on a quarterly basis. (The author wishes to thank Warren Heller of Veribanc for his generosity in making these analyses available.)
Notes: Veribanc's data base consists of all thrifts that file a quarterly call report with FSLIC. With minor exceptions, this is the set of FSLIC-insured thrifts.
Operating loss rates are sensitive to trends in market interest rates. In particular, interest-rate increases observed in late 1988 and early 1989 should push up the number of firms recorded in the first three columns during 1988.4 and 1989.1.

Table 3-3 INCOME, CAPITAL, AND REAL ESTATE OWNED RECORDED FOR INSOLVENT THRIFTS, 1987–88, BY QUARTER ($ Million)

Category of Insolvency and Quarter	Income for the Quarter	RAP Net Worth	GAAP-like Net Worth	Tangible Net Worth	Real Estate Owned
1. RAP-Insolvent S&Ls					
1987.1	−1,597	−9,134	−12,552	−18,687	6,897
1987.2	−2,205	−11,226	−14,531	−20,813	8,121
1987.3	−2,291	−13,708	−17,581	−24,398	10,941
1987.4	−3,204	−15,953	−20,033	−25,829	12,272
1988.1	−4,501	−20,447	−26,328	−32,494	15,348
1988.2	−4,455	−23,059	−29,113	−37,041	16,797
1988.3	−2,321	−15,688	−20,478	−23,494	11,426
2. GAAP-like Insolvent S&Ls					
1987.1	−1,426	−1,201	−20,925	−33,623	11,358
1987.2	−2,727	−1,160	−23,533	−35,605	13,618
1987.3	−2,475	−3,956	−26,012	−36,761	15,954
1987.4	−3,856	−6,885	−29,309	−39,430	17,737
1988.1	−4,681	−12,003	−33,705	−43,369	18,966
1988.2	−4,676	−15,020	−36,244	−47,692	19,812
1988.3	−2,629	−8,110	−27,123	−36,300	16,145

Identifying and Understanding FSLIC Mistakes 83

3. S&Ls with Negative Tangible Net Worth ("Tangible-Insolvent S&Ls")

1987.1	−1,260	10,694	−16,714	−40,127	13,635
1987.2	−2,692	9,696	−17,985	−42,260	15,784
1987.3	−2,598	6,597	−20,211	−43,039	18,222
1987.4	−3,787	5,852	−22,432	−46,493	19,856
1988.1	−4,610	−1,697	−29,254	−50,890	21,210
1988.2	−4,682	−5,880	−31,715	−55,190	21,840
1988.3	−2,675	−2,458	−24,787	−62,956	22,899

Source: Supplements to the Veribanc reports which were the source for table 3-2. These supplements are available only for the seven quarters shown in this table. (Again, the author wishes to express gratitude to Warren Heller for providing this material.)

Table 3-4 BALLPARK ESTIMATE OF THE ACCUMULATING IMBEDDED LOSS TO FSLIC THAT IS EMBODIED IN THE OPERATIONS OF GAAP-LIKE INSOLVENT AND TANGIBLE-INSOLVENT FIRMS, 1987–88, BY QUARTER ($ Million)

Quarter	Deficiency in Tangible Net Worth at GAAP-like Insolvent S&Ls	75 Percent of the Additional Deficiency in Tangible-Insolvent S&Ls	One-half of Real Estate Owned at Tangible-Insolvent S&Ls	Imbedded Loss to FSLIC in Tangible-Insolvent S&Ls[a]
1987.1	18,687	4,878	6,818	30,383
1987.2	20,813	4,991	7,892	33,696
1987.3	24,398	4,708	9,111	38,217
1987.4	25,829	5,297	9,928	41,054
1988.1	32,494	5,641	10,605	48,740
1988.2	37,041	5,624	10,920	53,585
1988.3	23,494	19,992	11,450	54,936

Source: Table 3-3.

a. Some of these imbedded losses came to be explicitly financed by FSLIC notes and guarantees, which by year-end 1988 totalled about $38 billion.

The average insolvency-resolution cost rate experienced by FSLIC over its lifetime in assistance cases is tracked in table 3-5. Although this rate fluctuates from year to year, it has trended sharply upward during the last five years as the regulatory-gambling theory would predict. During 1987 and 1988 when the rate of insolvency resolution stepped up, FSLIC's official estimate of its resolution cost averaged roughly 33 percent of assets. However, these estimates understate the cost to the U.S. Treasury in two ways. First, they neglect to measure the cost to taxpayers of the tax reductions passed through to acquirers. Second, in discounting future outflows, FSLIC calculations employ an interest rate that exceeds the Treasury's cost of funds by roughly a full percentage point.

For institutions that are insolvent on a GAAP-like basis, the percentage of assets that we may project to require a FSLIC-assisted resolution is virtually 100 percent. For the years 1982–87 and the second quarter of 1988, table 3-6 lists the number and total assets in FHLBB-designated GAAP-insolvent clients. Applying the insolvency-resolution cost rate observed year by year in table 3-5, the table produces an alternative measure of FSLIC's loss exposure in GAAP-insolvent thrifts alternative to the one reported in table 3-4. This analysis suggests that the calculation reported in table 3-4 is probably conservative.

Rates of Deposit Interest Paid by GAAP-Insolvent Thrifts

The level of explicit interest rates that GAAP-insolvent thrifts have recently been offering on certificates of deposit (CDs) of different denominations is tracked in table 3-7. Consistent with the corporate-finance theory of go-for-broke speculation, yields on large-denomination CDs tend to exceed yields on Treasury securities throughout the March 1987 to September 1988 period and to be higher for very large-denomination instruments. They also tend to exceed deposit rates paid by thrifts whose GAAP capital ratios exceed 6 percent. However, substantial differentials over Treasury yields are observed in June and December 1987 and in early 1988, even for thrifts identified as comparatively well-capitalized (i.e., those with GAAP capital ratios over 6 percent). At these times, it appears that differences in individual institutions' financial condition became less important than depositor worries about the repayment capacity of FSLIC itself. Doubt about FSLIC's capacity to make good its aggregate promises ebbs and flows in potentially dangerous ways. If, at a time when this concern is running at high tide, higher authorities should inadver-

Table 3-5 CALCULATION OF FSLIC'S AVERAGE INSOLVENCY-RESOLUTION COST RATE IN LIQUIDATIONS AND ASSISTED RESOLUTIONS, 1934–88

Year	Present Value of Insolvency Resolution Cost ($ million)[a]	Total Assets in Insolvencies Resolved ($ million)	Cost Rate (cents per dollar of assets)
1934–79	306.1	4,458.3	6.87
1980	166.6	1,457.6	11.43
1981	758.7	13,908.2	5.46
1982	803.3	17,662.1	4.55
1983	274.7	4,631.1	5.93
1984	742.6	5,080.2	14.62
1985	1,021.6	6,368.3	16.04
1986	3,065.0	12,455.1	24.61
1987	3,703.6	10,660.4	34.74
1988	31,179.5	100,659.9	30.98

Source: Calculated from FHLBB file table, "Attrition Among FSLIC-Insured Institutions: 1934–1988."

a. If we included the value of federal tax forgivenesses conveyed to acquirers of failed and failing thrifts and used the Treasury's cost of funds to discount future cash flows, the present value of the cost incurred in recent years would become substantially higher.

Table 3-6 ALTERNATIVE ESTIMATE OF FSLIC LOSSES IMBEDDED IN
THE OPERATIONS OF GAAP-INSOLVENT THRIFTS, 1982–88

Time Period	Number of Firms	Assets ($ billion)	Insolvency-Cost Resolution Rate (cents per dollar)	Estimate of FSLIC Loss Exposure ($ billion)
1982	237	67.8	4.55	3.08
1983	293	83.9	5.93	4.98
1984	445	115.5	14.62	16.89
1985	470	138.0	16.04	22.14
1986	471	137.2	24.61	33.76
1987	520	200.1	34.74	69.51
1988(2Q)	496	203.8	30.98	63.13

Source: Columns one and two: Barth and Bradley (1988, table 5).
Column three: table 3-5.

tently undermine FSLIC's credibility, a bureaucratic meltdown could
well be triggered.

THE IMPACT OF EXPANDED THRIFT POWERS: REFUTING A BAD RAP

The ways in which the balance sheets of GAAP-insolvent thrifts
diverged from those of GAAP-solvent ones after 1982 is highlighted
in table 3-8. The divergences fit our hypothesized pattern of lagged
accounting recognition of imbedded losses and of additional go-for-
broke plunging by insolvent firms into unfamiliar, tricky, or high-
risk activities. Nevertheless, the insolvent firms do not show dramatically different adjustments in the nature of the deregulated product lines they have constructed. GAAP-insolvent firms have put almost
the same percentages of their assets into commercial and consumer
loans as solvent thrifts have, and only slightly larger percentages into
commercial mortgages and exotic, hard-to-classify assets. However,
the nearly steady expansion the insolvent firms have experienced in
nonperforming assets and in negative GAAP net worth suggests that
these firms have been attracted disproportionately to the flow of
actuarially bad deals in new and old activities alike.

A very severe way to test this suggestion is to write off immediately
every dollar that GAAP-insolvent institutions place into newly authorized activities in excess of the benchmark percentage allocations

Table 3-7 EVIDENCE ON OFFERING INTEREST RATES ON THRIFT CDS, MARCH 1987 TO SEPTEMBER 1988

a. Interest Rates on Selected Financial Instruments

CD Offering Rates

		CDs under $80,000						For All GAAP-Insolvent Thrifts $80,000 < CD < $100,000			CDs over $100,000				
	No.	1–3 mo	3–6 mo	6–12 mo	1–2 yr	2–3 yr	>3 yr	1 mo	1–2 mo	2–3 mo	1 mo	1–2 mo	2–3 mo	3–6 mo	6–12 mo
3/87	476	5.84	6.16	6.49	6.74	6.97	7.18	6.18	6.25	6.45	5.99	6.06	6.18	6.49	6.73
6/87	498	6.23	6.75	7.19	7.44	7.68	7.87	7.04	7.18	7.50	6.66	6.81	7.01	7.35	7.70
9/87	511	6.49	7.10	7.55	7.83	8.04	8.21	7.11	7.30	7.64	6.82	7.04	7.28	7.63	7.98
12/87	520	6.69	7.34	7.80	8.07	8.25	8.38	7.22	7.47	7.83	7.21	7.32	7.61	7.95	8.18
3/88	509	6.44	6.95	7.41	7.71	7.90	8.00	6.53	6.72	6.96	6.66	6.75	6.95	7.30	7.59
6/88	498	6.61	7.14	7.56	7.87	8.03	8.20	6.72	6.95	7.26	6.90	7.02	7.24	7.64	7.93
9/88	433	7.02	7.74	8.15	8.37	8.47	8.58	7.31	7.49	7.84	7.50	7.61	7.84	8.28	8.57

Yields on U.S. Treasury Securities

	3 mo	6 mo	1 yr	2 yr	3 yr	5 yr	1 mo	2 mo	3 mo	1 mo	2 mo	3 mo	6 mo	1 yr
3/87	5.77	5.82	6.13	6.51	6.72	6.93	5.37	5.56	5.77	5.37	5.56	5.77	5.82	6.13
6/87	5.94	6.32	6.78	7.51	7.77	7.97	5.45	5.72	5.94	5.45	5.72	5.94	6.32	6.78
9/87	6.75	7.21	7.81	8.52	8.84	9.11	6.49	6.67	6.75	6.49	6.67	6.75	7.21	7.81
12/87	5.90	6.58	7.15	7.82	8.08	8.38	3.51	5.05	5.90	3.51	5.05	5.90	6.58	7.15
3/88	5.88	6.30	6.78	7.42	7.65	8.02	5.50	5.81	5.88	5.50	5.81	5.88	6.30	6.78
6/88	6.76	7.08	7.52	8.05	8.22	8.47	6.20	6.48	6.76	6.20	6.48	6.76	7.08	7.52
9/88	7.54	7.91	8.18	8.52	8.62	8.73	7.17	7.47	7.54	7.17	7.47	7.54	7.91	8.18

b. *Differentials between Thrift CD Rates and Treasury Yields*
For All GAAP-Insolvent Thrifts

No.	CDs under $80,000						$80,000 < CD < $100,000			CDs over $100,000				
	1–3 mo	3–6 mo	6–12 mo	1–2 yr	2–3 yr	>3 yr	1 mo	1–2 mo	2–3 mo	1 mo	1–2 mo	2–3 mo	3–6 mo	6–12 mo
3/87 476	0.07	0.34	0.36	0.23	0.25	0.25	0.81	0.69	0.68	0.62	0.50	0.41	0.67	0.60
6/87 498	0.29	0.43	0.41	-0.07	-0.09	-0.10	1.59	1.46	1.56	1.21	1.09	1.07	1.03	0.92
9/87 511	-0.26	-0.11	-0.26	-0.69	-0.80	-0.90	0.62	0.63	0.89	0.33	0.37	0.53	0.42	0.17
12/87 520	0.79	0.76	0.65	0.25	0.17	0.00	3.71	2.42	1.93	3.70	2.27	1.71	1.37	1.03
3/88 509	0.56	0.65	0.63	0.29	0.25	-0.02	1.03	0.91	1.08	1.16	0.94	1.07	1.00	0.81
6/88 498	-0.15	0.06	0.04	-0.18	-0.19	-0.27	0.52	0.47	0.50	0.70	0.54	0.48	0.56	0.41
9/88 433	-0.52	-0.17	-0.03	-0.15	-0.15	-0.15	0.14	0.02	0.30	0.33	0.14	0.30	0.37	0.39

For Thrifts with GAAP Capital Ratios Over 6%

No.	CDs under $80,000						$80,000 < CD < $100,000			CDs over $100,000				
	1–3 mo	3–6 mo	6–12 mo	1–2 yr	2–3 yr	>3 yr	1 mo	1–2 mo	2–3 mo	1 mo	1–2 mo	2–3 mo	3–6 mo	6–12 mo
3/87 1261	-0.09	0.17	0.18	0.04	0.10	0.21	0.44	0.28	0.15	0.51	0.36	0.20	0.31	0.25
6/87 1304	0.02	0.17	0.21	-0.33	-0.34	-0.28	0.77	0.58	0.49	0.89	0.68	0.53	0.49	0.39
9/87 1326	-0.41	-0.32	-0.41	-0.81	-0.89	-0.91	0.11	-0.01	0.10	0.15	0.08	0.11	0.03	-0.22
12/87 1318	0.62	0.69	0.58	0.17	0.16	0.06	3.28	1.80	1.20	3.39	1.94	1.26	0.98	0.77
3/88 1325	0.42	0.58	0.52	0.18	0.21	0.06	0.92	0.74	0.78	0.97	0.71	0.74	0.69	0.54
6/88 1334	-0.32	-0.02	0.01	-0.26	-0.18	-0.20	0.37	0.22	0.12	0.64	0.45	0.26	0.30	0.18
9/88 1370	-0.67	-0.32	-0.14	-0.30	-0.25	-0.20	0.03	-0.19	-0.05	0.19	-0.02	0.04	0.05	0.10

Source: Hirschhorn (1988).

Table 3-8 DIFFERENCES IN THE RATIOS OF SELECTED BALANCE-SHEET POSITIONS TO TOTAL ASSETS AT GAAP-SOLVENT AND GAAP-INSOLVENT THRIFTS INSURED BY FSLIC, 1982 TO MID-1988

	1982	1983	1984	1985	1986	1987	1988(2Q)
Gross Assets (in $ billion)							
Solvent firms	649.4	775.6	910.6	981.9	1,075.5	1,103.9	1,137.1
Insolvent firms	67.8	83.9	115.5	138.0	137.2	200.1	203.8
Percentage of Total Assets Placed in:							
Residential Mortgages							
Solvent firms	n.r.	n.r.	n.r.	49.6	46.4	46.3	46.5
Insolvent firms	n.r.	n.r.	n.r.	43.1	36.4	31.3	30.4
Commercial Mortgages							
Solvent firms	n.r.	n.r.	n.r.	12.0	10.7	9.9	9.6
Insolvent firms	n.r.	n.r.	n.r.	12.7	17.2	14.5	13.8
Consumer Loans							
Solvent firms	2.7	2.9	3.2	3.9	4.1	4.4	4.6
Insolvent firms	2.9	3.3	4.2	4.7	5.0	3.8	3.5
Commercial Loans							
Solvent firms	0.0	0.0	1.1	1.5	1.8	1.7	1.8
Insolvent firms	0.0	0.0	0.9	1.3	2.3	1.9	1.7
Repossessed Assets							
Solvent firms	0.4	0.5	0.5	0.7	0.9	0.9	0.9
Insolvent firms	0.5	0.6	0.9	2.1	4.7	7.8	8.7
Real Estate Held							
Solvent firms	0.4	0.5	0.6	0.6	0.6	0.4	0.4
Insolvent firms	0.1	0.3	0.4	1.2	1.7	2.1	1.9
Hard-to-Classify Assets							
Solvent firms	5.2	5.4	6.2	6.4	6.0	5.8	5.6
Insolvent firms	10.7	10.0	9.3	9.8	9.3	8.0	8.0

Direct Investments							
Solvent firms	1.2	1.5	2.3	2.7	2.4	2.2	2.3
Insolvent firms	1.2	1.7	1.7	2.9	4.1	4.4	4.3
Junk Bonds							
Solvent firms	n.r.	n.r.	n.r.	0.6	0.7	1.1	1.1
Insolvent firms	n.r.	n.r.	n.r.	0.1	0.1	0.2	0.6
Nonperforming Assets[b]							
Solvent firms	4.0	4.3	4.6	5.0	5.5	5.3	5.1
Insolvent firms	10.0	9.9	9.7	13.2	18.9	22.0	21.7
Net Worth (RAP)							
Solvent firms	4.0	4.3	4.1	4.8	5.6	5.8	5.8
Insolvent firms	1.2	1.5	1.6	0.9	−4.8	−8.5	−11.8
Net Worth (GAAP)							
Solvent firms	3.6	3.8	3.5	4.2	4.8	5.1	5.1
Insolvent firms	−3.4	−3.2	−3.2	−4.1	−8.6	−10.9	−14.0
Large Time Deposits							
Solvent firms	9.1	11.8	12.6	11.2	10.9	11.1	11.2
Insolvent firms	6.3	7.1	8.1	6.7	7.6	6.4	5.7
Brokered Time Deposits[a]							
Solvent firms	1.3	4.1	4.9	4.3	4.0	5.4	5.2
Insolvent firms	0.6	1.3	2.2	2.0	3.7	4.9	5.3
Repurchase Agreements[a]							
Solvent firms	3.5	3.6	5.3	4.7	5.8	6.6	6.6
Insolvent firms	3.4	3.0	3.5	2.9	1.9	9.6	9.2

Source: Barth and Bradley (1988).

[a]Figures are stated as a percentage of total liabilities.

[b]Nonperforming assets are defined as the sum of repossessed assets, deferred net losses (gains) on loans and other assets, goodwill and "other" intangible assets, and delinquent loans.

n.r. = not reported.

Table 3-9 COMPARISON OF DIFFERENCES IN THE CAPITAL
POSITIONS OF GAAP-SOLVENT AND GAAP-INSOLVENT
THRIFTS WITH MAXIMAL HYPOTHETICAL LOSSES ON
DIFFERENCES IN NONTRADITIONAL LOANS AND
INVESTMENTS, 1982–88(2Q) (percent of total assets)

	1982	1983	1984	1985	1986	1987	1988(2Q)
Commercial Mortgages	—	—	—	0.7	6.5	4.6	4.2
Consumer Loans	0.2	0.4	1.0	0.8	0.9	− 0.6	− 1.1
Commercial Loans	0.0	0.0	− 0.2	− 0.2	0.5	0.2	− 0.1
Real Estate Held	− 0.3	− 0.2	− 0.2	0.6	1.1	1.7	1.5
Hard-to-Classify Assets	5.5	4.6	3.1	3.4	3.3	2.2	2.4
Direct Investments	0.0	− 0.4	− 0.6	0.2	1.7	2.2	2.0
Junk Bonds	—	—	—	− 0.5	− 0.6	− 0.9	− 0.5
Hypothetical Difference in GAAP Net Worth	5.4	4.4	3.1	5.0	13.4	8.4	8.4
Actual Difference in GAAP Net Worth	7.0	7.0	6.7	8.3	13.4	16.0	19.1

Source: Calculated from table 3.8.

held by solvent thrifts. Because the worthlessness of a bad investment
is seldom complete and never immediately visible, this is a very
extreme assumption. Table 3-9 shows that, even using this extreme
assumption about the extent and timing of asset writedowns, except
in 1986 differential investments can only partly account for observed
differences in GAAP net worth. Moreover, in 1987 and 1988(2Q) the
percent of the capital differential that this method can account for
falls substantially. Something else was obviously going on.

The problem with the deregulation hypothesis is not just that differences in the extent of newly authorized dealings cannot account for
more than a fraction of insolvent thrifts' proportionately greater losses.
Many of the losses insolvent thrifts sustained as commercial lenders
or direct investors in real estate development could have been booked
as go-for-broke real estate lending under pre-1980 and pre-1982 rules.
The predominant feature of the sourest loans and investments made
is simply that they allowed thrift accountants to realize front-loaded
fees at the time the deal was booked.

SUMMARY AND TRANSITION

The economic insolvency of the FSLIC and its zombie clients has
been systematically covered up by smoke-and-mirrors accounting.

This coverup has kept the imbedded losses out of the explicit federal budget, so that politicians and regulators have not yet had to present the bill for the insolvencies to federal taxpayers.

The costs to taxpayers inherent in these policies of coverup and deferral are disturbingly high and rapidly accelerating. The higher these costs became, the harder it became to keep the coverup from unraveling. As long as deposit-insurance bureaucrats are free to under-reserve for losses they are responsible for covering, a financial and bureaucratic meltdown of the deposit-insurance funds remains a possibility.

Chapter four seeks to answer two questions. First, what made Congress and FSLIC officials so slow to perceive how perverse managerial incentives become at a decapitalized firm? Second, once the incentive conflict was understood, what made federal officials so reluctant to design and install an adequate set of counterincentives?

Note

1. This section draws extensively on Kane (1983).

References

Barth, James R., and Michael G. Bradley. 1988. "Thrift Deregulation and Federal Deposit Insurance." Washington: Office of Economic Policy Research, Federal Home Loan Bank Board (November).

Brumbaugh, R. Dan, Jr. 1988. *Thrifts Under Siege.* Cambridge, Mass.: Ballinger Publishing Co.

Hirschhorn, Eric. 1988. "Interest Rates on Thrift Certificates of Deposit." Washington: Office of Policy and Economc Research, Federal Home Loan Bank Board (December).

Jensen, Michael C., and William H. Meckling. 1975. "Theory of the Firm: Managerial Behavior, Agency Costs, and Ownership Structure." *Journal of Financial Economics* 3 (June), pp. 305–60.

Kane, Edward J. 1983. "The Role of Government in the Thrift Industry's Net-Worth Crisis." in George Benston (ed.) *Financial Services: The Changing Institutions and Government Policy,* Englewood Cliffs: Prentice-Hall, Inc. for the American Assembly, pp. 156–84.

————. 1985. *The Gathering Crisis in Federal Deposit Insurance.* Cambridge, Mass.: MIT Press, 1985

Wagner, Richard E. 1986. "The Agent-Principal Relationship in the Public Sector," in Karl Brunner and R. E. Wagner (eds.) *The Growth of Government.* Rochester: Center for Research in Government Policy & Business, University of Rochester, pp. 37–53.

Chapter Four

SOCIALLY PERVERSE INCENTIVES CONFRONTING THRIFT REGULATORS

Environmental change exposes state and federal deposit-insurance funds to a number of risks.[1] The purpose of this chapter is to understand what these risks are.

During the last 25 years, new financial instruments and new financial technologies have proliferated. Other things equal, these environmental changes and accompanying macroeconomic instability increased insured institutions' risk exposure. At the same time, these changes in the financial and economic environments enhanced discretionary opportunities for aggressive managers of insured institutions to increase their risk exposure even further. Particularly for decapitalized firms, environmental change interacted with weaknesses in historical-cost accounting to increase insured institutions' capacities to conceal their accumulating losses from the public eye.

To the extent that aggressive thrift managers could actually conceal their unbooked losses from FSLIC monitors merely by not booking them, a massive capital shortage may be said in part—but only in part—to have sneaked up on deposit-insurance officials. The full attack, which victimized not only the managers of FSLIC but also the managers of several state-sponsored deposit-insurance schemes, puts one in mind of the raids that renegades and desperadoes used to make on frontier towns.

THE LOOTING OF FSLIC

In the last half of the nineteenth century, gangs of masked gunmen roamed the Southwest and other frontier areas. Opposed and eventually tamed by a collection of local sheriffs and federal marshals, their favorite targets were railroads and banks. In the 1980s, with much the same energy, gangs of raiders have attacked thrifts in these and other regions and emptied their supporting deposit-insurance fund. But this time around, the looters have not had to use guns or masks. This is because they have been able to corrupt or politically hamstring the state and federal officials who should in principle have opposed them.

The weapon these maskless holdup men have used to face down 20th-century lawmen is what I refer to throughout the book as the zombie thrift. A zombie thrift, of course, is a decapitalized or economically insolvent savings institution that a well-armed and truly heroic regulator would feel impelled to plant in boot hill unless its managers agreed to recapitalize it promptly.

In permitting an unrecapitalized zombie firm to stay in operation, authorities replace the departed stockholder-contributed or mutual capital of the firm by what are effectively government equity investments. However, these investments are poorly structured and misleadingly labeled. They are poorly structured because they claim too little of the firm's upside potential for gain. They are misleadingly labeled because they are generally written, not as stock but in the form of FSLIC guarantees of various types.

The distorted or "undead" character of the economic life these firms enjoy creates incentives for them to pursue socially "evil" funding, lending, and investment strategies. These strategies are evil because on average they impose additional losses on the FSLIC insurance fund (Kane 1987). Effectively, these firms feed on the markets and profits of well-capitalized competitors, threatening to turn many of them into zombies too.

A contagious decapitalization of competing firms occurs in two ways. First, zombies' desire to place large risky bets in a hurry leads them to bid down industry profit margins by paying unsustainably high rates of deposit interest and accepting unsustainably low rates of interest on loans and investments. Second, the average losses these bets impose on the deposit-insurance fund raise the insurance premiums that surviving institutions must eventually pay.

Although other factors have been contributory, modern government officials' unwillingness or inability to shoot it out with the operators of zombie thrifts has been the decisive factor in the ballooning of the FSLIC/industry mess. To understand how to avoid a repetition of this mistake in the future, it is necessary to understand how rational public officials came to adopt such perverse policies in the first place and what could have persuaded them to hold what proved to be spectacularly unsuccessful policies in place for so long.

Returning to the metaphor of the Old West, we may transform this issue into something that could fit on a bumper sticker or tee shirt. The question is, "Where Have All the Heroes Gone?" Why have modern government officials (Members of Congress, presidents, and top regulatory officials) behaved so much less heroically, and in some cases less honorably, than the lawmen of yesteryear?

The answer to such a question must be sought in differences in operative incentives. In the Old West, lawmen could arm themselves appropriately and were paid rewards in money and reputation that varied more or less proportionately with the benefits to society of taking a particular desperado out of circulation. The names of the officials who ended the outlaw careers of Billy the Kid and Jesse James remain famous even after 100 years. Frontier regulators built their careers by curbing wrongful behavior and punishing enemies of society. Posters that proclaimed "Wanted: Dead or Alive" made it clear that higher officials had decided to subordinate a career bankrobber's right to life to the rights of the citizenry as a whole.

Modern depository supervisors and regulators, in contrast, find heroic action to be a form of professional suicide. They know the courts might rule that attempting to close a horde of zombie firms far exceeds the range of their underpowered administrative weapons, and that such strong action in any case would threaten to provoke personally ruinous flows of contrary political pressure focused through Congress. The ensuing fuss would also force them to reveal the depth of the hidden economic insolvency into which they and their predecessors had led their insurance fund.

Congressional pressure for forbearance can be compared to a western marshal's having to worry about his gun backfiring or being shot in the back by an alleged colleague in the midst of a gunfight. The root problem is that delaying definitive action on insurance-fund losses tends in the short run to benefit politicians. Firms threatened with heavy burdens from supervisory and regulatory discipline feel a need to build and exercise whatever political clout they can muster. Leaving the distribution of bailout costs unsettled enhances elected politicians' capacity to milk troubled individual constituents and industry political action committees. To my mind, intimidating political backshooting is prototypically exemplified by House Speaker Jim Wright's well-publicized efforts to forestall the closure of a series of deeply insolvent Texas S&Ls and by the success that the $5.5 billion Lincoln Savings and Loan had in having the Federal Home Loan Bank of San Francisco ordered off its case.

Congress and the Office of Management and Budget (OMB) left FSLIC short not only of explicit financial capital, but also of the

human resources and legal authority needed to carry out its responsibility to taxpayers. FSLIC's resource shortages trace in part to effective lobbying activity by the U.S. League of Savings Associations,
whose spokespersons took advantage of the ideological ascendancy
of concerns about getting the government off the backs of businesses
and reducing the explicit costs of government. Particularly frustrat-
ing was Edwin Gray's unsuccessful battle to get OMB approval for
750 new examiner slots, which began belatedly in calendar 1984
(Binstein 1988; and Strunk and Case 1988).

With Congress and sitting presidents unwilling to supply FSLIC
with the financial and human resources needed to round up and
bury its zombies and thereby to restore its own solvency, the FSLIC
braintrust maintained it had little choice but to gamble almost as
energetically as its unnaturally alive clients on unlikely and risky
get-well schemes and thinly capitalized boomerang financings. FSLIC
officials' scope for action was continually narrowed by direct industry pressure, by the extent of past coverups, and by constraints
imposed on their activity by elected officials.

CHANGES IN FSLIC'S REGULATORY STRATEGY

FSLIC officials have proved unable or unwilling to close more than
a fraction of their economically insolvent clients. Economic insolvency occurs when the market value of a firm's assets falls short of
the market value of its nonequity liabilities. Because the GAAP information framework permits unrealized losses to be deferred and
converted into below-market future earnings, the 1980s surge in GAAP
insolvencies reflects in lagged fashion an epidemic of economic or
market-value insolvencies brought about much earlier by the post-
1965 upward trend in interest rates (Kane 1981). Chapter two describes the process by which the number of FSLIC-initiated insolvency resolutions increasingly lagged behind the number of FSLIC
clients judged to be insolvent on the basis of GAAP accounting. It
also identifies some of the weaker forms of discipline FSLIC officials
often used as substitutes for recapitalization. Under many of these
forms of administrative penalties, the managers that oversaw the
decapitalization were actually left in charge. Even when these managers were replaced with new ones, incentives to devise and undertake uncontrolled ways of making risky financial plays remained
very strong.

Except for 1976, before 1980 only a few FSLIC clients became GAAP-insolvent in any year. During this era, voluntary recapitalization and supervisory insolvency-resolution efforts kept the number of GAAP insolvencies small. By 1980, however, a succession of years of low reported earnings had begun to undermine GAAP's effectiveness in cloaking economic insolvencies at individual thrifts.

FHLBB regulatory strategy adapted to this development in two stages. In the 1980–82 period, officials greatly increased their insolvency-resolution activity. By late-1981, the vigorous efforts of the then-head of FSLIC (H. Brent Beesley) to promote supervisory mergers caused industry critics to liken him to the *Marvel Comics* villain, "Doctor Doom." But, despite the heightened pace of FSLIC insolvency resolution, new GAAP insolvencies developed faster than FSLIC officials resolved each year's carryover caseload. Moreover, as discussed in chapter two, the amount of assets held in recognized problem institutions increased rapidly.

If the argument could be restricted only to the trend in insolvencies, one might be able to build a case that, during 1980–82, FSLIC forbearance was driven by prior blindness to the dangers of guaranteeing economically insolvent clients and bureaucratic lags inherent in gearing an agency up to handle a surging problem. At least in these years, the number of insolvency resolutions expanded at about the same rate as the number of GAAP-insolvent clients. However, even in this era, FSLIC's capacity to resolve what was already understood to be a $100 billion worth of economic insolvencies was constrained by its lack of resources.

In addition, FSLIC managers appear not to have recognized the need to expand their examination force to handle the increased complexity of thrift operations allowed by the 1980 and 1982 financial reform legislation. In 1983, we observe a sharp fall in the ratio of resolutions to the number of firms identified as GAAP-insolvent at the previous yearend. At the same time, we see the beginnings of a four-year expansion in the use of other varieties of client discipline. The turning point appears to have developed sometime in 1982, when FHLBB officials lowered capital requirements to 3 percent (Barth and Bradley 1988) and adopted the dangerously lenient RAP system for measuring client capital.

In making these adjustments, authorities promoted the overly optimistic hypothesis that the decline in interest rates that began in mid-1982 and the October 1982 Garn-St Germain Act had ended the industry's tough times. In a paper drafted during this interval, Carron (1983, p. 30) offered the following more careful assessment:

Although many thrift institutions succumbed to their plight, the thrift industry has been rescued. Repercussions from the events of the past few years will continue to be felt, even with continued moderation of interest rates. The backlog of merger cases ensures further consolidation, and the net worth assistance program will require close supervision of large numbers of firms for up to ten years. But the crisis is over.

The repercussions Carron describes turned out to be nastier than he anticipated precisely because the close supervision he anticipated was not forthcoming. Given the decision to adopt RAP accounting, the FHLBB's monitoring effort needed to expand appropriately to offset the temptations that figured to lure its insolvent and near-insolvent clients into go-for-broke lending and investment plays. Two important problems with FSLIC monitoring procedures were the long interval of time that could pass between examinations and, before 1984, the extent to which these examinations focused on compliance with specific regulations rather than on an institution's overall financial condition. Wang, Sauerhaft, and Edwards (1987, p. 5) report that several hundred FSLIC clients had not been examined even once between January 1984 and July 1986. Among the 2,984 thrifts that were examined in this period, 935 had last been examined in 1984, 1,772 in 1985, and only 277 in 1986. Despite the burgeoning of the various kinds of insolvencies explained in chapter three, until 1984 FHLBB authorities remained relatively insensitive to their need to expand their examination force and to modernize the examination process.

Incredibly, examination and supervisory resources declined in 1983 and 1984 (see table 4-1), precisely when the economics of FSLIC's exposure to zombie risk taking was expanding and becoming harder to assess. This is true whether we measure these resources by the number of staff members assigned to these functions or by the ratio of the bureau's examination-supervisory budget to the value of assets in FSLIC-insured institutions. Table 4-1 also indicates that the field examination staff actually continued to decline (because of OMB efforts to enforce Congress' false notion of economy in government) even into early 1985, and continued to expand inadequately even after the clever bureaucratic maneuver of moving examination personnel from FSLIC to the District Home Loan Banks, whose budgets do not go through the OMB and congressional review process.

The FHLBB's 1987 Annual Report indicates that the frequency of examination had increased by 1987, with nonproblem institutions being examined every 17 months and problem institutions examined every 12 months. These data refer to site examinations. When one

Table 4-1 ESTIMATE OF SIZE OF FSLIC'S EXAMINATION AND
SUPERVISORY RESOURCES IN SELECTED YEARS, 1936–86

Year	Field Examination Positions at District Offices	Examination and Supervisory Resources		Assets in FSLIC-Insured Institutions ($ billion)
		Staff	Budget ($ million)	
1936	155	—	—	—
1946	262	—	—	—
1956	510	—	—	—
1966	755	—	—	—
1976	815	—	—	—
1977	813	—	—	—
1978	919	—	—	—
1979	919	1,282	41.0	568.1
1980	919	1,308	49.8	620.6
1981	937	1,385	52.8	658.5
1982	917	1,379	57.3	686.2
1983	891	1,368	62.5	813.8
1984	875	1,337	67.0	977.5
July 1985[a]	747	—	—	—
1985	1,006	1,990	108.8	1,070.0
1986	1,524	2,986	168.5	1,163.8
1987	—	3,258	207.6	1,250.8

Source: Column one: 1936–84: Strunk and Case (1988), pp. 138 and 139;
1985 figures from FHLBB, 1985 Annual Report, p. 21; 1986: Strunk and
Case (1988), p. 148.
Other columns: Barth and Bradley (1988, table 8).
a. Date of the FHLBB's administrative transfer of the examination
function to District Banks.

recognizes how quickly an aggressive firm can expand its risk taking,
electronic reporting and automated analysis could and should be
adapted to control even further the risk of loss that site-examination
lags impose on FSLIC.

A MODEL OF CHANGES IN REGULATORY INCENTIVES

It is instructive to think of thrift regulators as being employed under
a two-part compensation scheme. The explicit salary a competent

regulator is offered for his or her term in office is clearly lower than the salary the same person could earn in the private sector. However, since such a person chooses the public sector job, we may presume that the gap is more or less filled by what economists call implicit wages. Implicit wages consist of the nonpecuniary pleasures of exercising the powers conferred by high office and an additional and deferred increment in wages that accrues in postgovernment employment. The idea that this analysis seeks to emphasize is that completing a term of successful service in a top government post enhances an individual's resumé and professional reputation. This professional "blessing" or resumé enhancement promises to permit an undisgraced official to command a higher wage in postgovernment employment than would have been available in the absence of his or her period of government service.

To the extent that an official can hide adverse information about the quality of his or her job performance, serious conflicts of interest can develop between his or her career interests and responsibility to the general taxpayer whom we may deem to be an official's ultimate principal. Assuming that incremental deferred wages depend on public *perceptions* of the quality of an individual's public service creates a sensitivity to just, as well as unjust, public criticism.

Possibilities for covering up adverse information about fund performance are a temptation that constantly confronts even the most honorable deposit-insurance regulator. Assuming that insured institutions perennially develop new and partly unforecastable ways to shift risk onto their insurance fund, we may suppose that these temptations lure at least some deposit-insurance regulators through a time-consuming cycle of three regulatory regimes. It is convenient to name these regimes as follows:

1. Slow but open regulatory responses to client innovations;
2. At least partially well-meaning denial of reputation-threatening problem situations;
3. Grudging admittance of the truth about what needs to be done to cure the insolvent deposit-insurance fund's increasingly obvious problems.

Incentive-crossover points occur that move official policy across adjacent regimes. The attractiveness of changing the policy regime depends on:

☐ the extent to which a regulator's insurance fund is economically insolvent;

□ how easy or hard it is to hide the size of the problem from the general public; and
□ the reluctance of elected officials to support an agency's efforts to raise effective premiums and expand its monitoring and liquidation effort.

My analysis of the FSLIC mess portrays the fund's insolvency as initially sneaking up on honorable administrators. It should be emphasized, however, that knowable information that implied they should be taking strong action lay around their offices in the form of accounting data formatted in a hard-to-assimilate fashion. Analyses of the dangers economically insolvent clients pose to a deposit insurer were also present in bureau libraries. Articles and books in the economics and finance literature clarifying this point include Meltzer (1967); Scott and Mayer (1971); Black, Miller, and Posner (1974); Merton (1978); Kareken and Wallace (1978); Buser, Chen, and Kane (1981); McCulloch (1981); Kane (1981); Guttentag and Herring (1982); Pyle (1983); and Kareken (1983). Ideas contained in the manuscripts of most of the 1981, 1982, and 1983 papers were presented earlier at industry conferences and circulated prior to publication in working-paper form.

That large implicit losses can be imposed on a government insurance fund without this fact being immediately recognized can be attributed to three factors:

□ weaknesses in the insurer's information and monitoring systems (some of which authorities may either deliberately or unconsciously foster as a way of creating blame-disbursement information-management options);
□ unanticipated or unappreciated changes that develop in the macroeconomic environment and in the technology of institutional risk taking; and
□ humankind's well-established psychological propensity to resist unpleasant facts when they first emerge.

Once a fund's unbooked losses become very large, it is hard for managers of a deposit-insurance bureau to tighten monitoring or insolvency resolution sufficiently without being perceived at least in part to be causing the industry the very problems they are seeking to cure. Fear of undermining public confidence in a weak fund and triggering a wave of contagious failures tends to inhibit strong supervisory action. Unless Congress signals its willingness to extend the insurer's right to restructure premiums and to supply the resources necessary to undertake the monitoring and client-recapitalization activities necessary to protect the fund, a regulator's short-term responsibilities and post-government career interests can best be served by covering up the magnitude of the fund's insolvency. Efforts to keep the serious nature of the industry's and its insurance fund's problems out of the press may be rationalized as "necessary" to prevent runs and a general loss of depositor confidence. But maintaining the fiction that an insolvent fund is okay requires a policy of increased capital-requirement forbearance. Such a policy favors decapitalized clients over the taxpayers (including well-capitalized institutions) who must realistically anticipate being asked eventually to fill in the hole in the insurance fund's finances.

Adopting a coverup strategy helps top insurance officials to keep politicians from criticizing them publicly. At the same time, it amounts to gambling that they can either convince Congress privately of the need to deal with the fund's resource shortage, or if not, still make a reputationally clean getaway to another job before a fund meltdown takes place. When faced with hidden problems, a self-interested regulator may want to avoid a bad press far more than he or she wants to avoid myopic policies. Nevertheless, it is difficult for a successive line of agency heads indefinitely to hide relevant information. Although agencies are not subject to takeover discipline, officials' capacity to misrepresent agency income and net worth is limited by the press and GAO auditors. Although GAO auditors are subject to short-run political pressures too, they are a long-run source of accounting discipline. However loose accounting discipline may be in the short run, over long periods it is a force for truth. An insurer's deception cannot go on forever. Before a great many years, someone in the line of succession will find it in his or her career interest to accept the political costs of trying to raise insurance premiums, intensify monitoring efforts, and step up the pace of insolvency resolution. However, this agency head may find that the legislature or higher administrative officials to whom he or she reports are unwilling to accept the political heat generated by acknowledging the insolvency and incurring the increased tax burden or government deficit this strategy implies. For example, in 1984–85, OMB and congressional leaders fought former FHLBB Chairman Ed Gray when he finally decided it would be wise to move in the direction of acknowledging the problem.

ROLE OF AGENCY COSTS

As executives of what is effectively a corporate subsidiary of the federal government, FSLIC officials have been delegated only a narrow range of control over FSLIC's premiums and monitoring effort. The right to make substantial adjustments in these variables has been reserved by Congress. This means that when changing circumstances require a dramatic realignment in pricing and regulatory strategy, FSLIC officials must persuade Congress and OMB to go along with them.

In recent years, Congress has fought rather than assisted well-intentioned FSLIC efforts both to increase its monitoring efforts and to employ the fruit of its existing effort to force the recapitalization of zombie and near-zombie firms. By constraining the agency's budget for monitoring and insolvency-resolution activities, politicians have been able to postpone politically tough decisions indefinitely. This has protected a number of politicians' own careers in the short run, at the same time as keeping open the threat of reconfiguring industry subsidies allows them to milk troubled constituents and industry political action committees more effectively.

Congressional resistance to reform raises the reputational and career costs to FSLIC officials of admitting the truth. More generally, congressional efforts to forestall adjustments proposed by FSLIC managers intensify the conflict of interest between these managers and federal taxpayers. The imperfect budget discipline under which government enterprises operate accounts for explicit revenues and costs, but permits enterprise managers to conceal implicit revenues and costs whenever they find it useful to do so. Congress's focus on restraining the explicit expenses of FSLIC encourages its managers to develop substitutes for explicit outlays that do not affect its current annual budget.

This informational defect in FSLIC's accounting system helps FSLIC officials to tolerate a parallel weakness in the accounting requirements they impose on client thrifts. By not requiring FSLIC's clients to report their best estimates of their own implicit losses as they occur, FSLIC officials leave themselves with only an imperfect perception of the permanent level of insolvency resolution costs that are actually imbedded in client operations.

Delays in perceiving surges in FSLIC's implicit loss exposure account for some of this bureau's delay in adjusting its monitoring effort and premiums to the levels that would have maximized the

value of FSLIC as an economic enterprise. Even far-sighted and in-
centive-unconflicted managers would be subject to this form of regulatory lag. However, as I have argued repeatedly, deposit-insurance
officials are unconflicted value-maximizers only if the scheme by
which they are compensated for their services makes it in their self-
interest to act this way. If the possibility of hiding adverse information exists, what an enterprise's officials decide to maximize depends also on the incentives conveyed by the manner in which they
are compensated (cf. Myers and Majluf 1984; Narayanan 1985; Campbell and Marino 1988).

The theory of principal-agent conflict leads us to interpret a set of
well-known, but longstanding imperfections in the accounting systems used by FSLIC and its clients as empirical evidence. The survival and repeated defense of such imperfections suggest that these
imperfections deliver benefits to politicians and/or FSLIC's top managers—benefits that are generated, of course, at the expense of taxpayers.

Assuming that politicians and FSLIC managers recognize the existence of its clients' hidden losses implies that they recognize, at
least unconsciously, that the capacity of clients to conceal their insolvency creates valuable deniability options by which authorities
can conceal FSLIC's weaknesses at least in part, and can shift blame
for them if and when these losses later surface publicly. Moreover,
the brevity of politicians' and FSLIC officials' anticipated term in
office may also tempt them to myopia. Losses that can be put off
until after they leave office can be virtually ignored.

AGENCY COSTS AND CONGRESSIONALLY MANDATED
CEILINGS ON TOP OFFICIALS' SALARIES

In federal service today, top officials accept below-market salaries
for their period of government service. For the purpose of this discussion, it is useful to refer to salaries as explicit compensation. For
most officials, the gap between this explicit compensation and the
market value of their services is filled in by implicit wages. Implicit
wages include all the nonpecuniary pleasures of high office—such
as the respect of other citizens, opportunities to promote one's ideological view of the world, or a chance to exercise power per se. They
also include another form of implicit wages, which I earlier termed
the "resumé-enhancement" effect of government service. This effect

consists of the elevation in salary an official expects to command in postgovernment employment, precisely because the perceived value of his or her human capital is enhanced or "blessed" by having adequately or more than adequately met the demands of a high government post. (The postgovernment career opportunities that have unfolded as a result of distinguished public service for Paul Volcker and Henry Kissinger dramatically exemplify the existence of this category of implicit compensation.)

It is reasonable to assume that the projected present value of explicit wages expected to be earned in postgovernment employment is an increasing function of: the official's inherent competence; the boons delivered to firms that an official may reasonably view as prospective employers; and the perceived quality of the official's performance in government service. We may define the true value of the official's performance as the change in the unobservable market value of the deposit-insurance enterprise during the official's time in office. The *perceived* value of this performance differs from the true value in three ways. First, the perceived market value of the enterprise at the time the official takes office is likely to have been overstated by his or her predecessor. Second, to the extent that clients can successfully conceal new risk taking, the official's best estimate at the time of his or her departure of the future costs of resolving client insolvencies is apt to be understated. Finally, to the extent that the official can suppress unfavorable information about the size of the agency's unresolved implicit losses, the public can be persuaded to believe that these costs are only a fraction of the value known by agency insiders.

The link between an official's reputation and postgovernment wages and his or her ability to manipulate public perceptions of his or her performance create incentives for information suppression. Such incentives make confrontations between the press and incumbent governments a perennial, worldwide fact of life.

As long as FSLIC's imbedded losses remain small, public relations efforts can probably paint minor adjustments in premiums or monitoring effort as cleverly enough designed to overcome adverse movements observed in measures of the enterprise's explicit deficits. However, when imbedded losses become large or deteriorate suddenly, it is impossible for a regulator to tighten monitoring and insolvency resolution activity sufficiently without being perceived to be aggravating industry problems. Career penalties for acknowledging unrealized losses, therefore, create the possibility of an incentive-crossover point at which an official's sense of honor becomes over-whelmed by the career benefits of covering up the magnitude of the agency's insolvency problems.

Self-interested regulatory forbearance is myopic for society. It worsens FSLIC losses in the long run because covering up fund and client insolvencies means permitting insolvent clients to operate.

For probably all FHLBB chairmen of the last 20 years, FSLIC's imbedded losses have increased during their term in office and politicians have interfered with their efforts to bring these losses under control. Congress has denied FSLIC not only the right to restructure premiums beyond imposing a blanket supplementary premium but also the resources required to undertake the monitoring and recapitalization activities truly needed to protect the fund. Hence, the only way each new set of top FHLBB officials could count upon obtaining a positive performance rating would have been by concealing, jointly with industry managers, a larger fraction of anticipated losses than their predecessors did.

Through mid-1987, thrift-industry lobbying generated disinformation that painted the industry's imbedded losses as if it were only a minor figure. This strategy raised the possibility that any realistic official acknowledgment of the size of FSLIC's shortage of explicit capital could precipitate a bureaucratic meltdown. Industry spokespersons stood ready to blame any straight-talking official for mishandling his or her post and for causing the large losses that he or she would be revealing. Introducing industry and congressional opposition to FSLIC efforts to acknowledge imbedded losses and to increase its premiums and monitoring effort forces an official to choose between continuing the coverup and embarking on a hard-to-predict and career-threatening course of reform.

At the same time, the longer a coverup goes on the harder it becomes to keep the deception going. First, not acknowledging implicit losses in a firm's accounts as they develop does not make them disappear. It simply defers their accounting recognition. Losses that have been deferred into the present from the past create a drag on the industry's and the insurance fund's ability to report positive current earnings. Second, permitting economically insolvent institutions to stay in operation tends on average to escalate the rate of growth of the insurance fund's imbedded losses over time (Barth, Brumbaugh and Sauerhaft 1986; Benston et al. 1986; Kane 1985, 1987). For decapitalized firms, the downside risk of speculative projects goes predominantly to the guarantor. Moreover, the eagerness with which such institutions bid for deposits and risky projects undermines the margins and market values even of the fund's healthy clients.

WHERE WE ARE NOW

By 1988, the "no-getaway" or truth-admittance cross-over point was reached. In 1987, officials of the U.S. League of Savings Associations, the GAO, and the FHLBB were willing to contend that a $10.8 billion reliquification of FSLIC would be adequate (e.g., Garcia 1988). All three parties have since drastically changed their tune, although delays in accounting recognition of imbedded losses continue to produce understatement. Economically solvent S&Ls have pressured the U.S. League to lobby for a taxpayer bailout. By year-end 1988, the FHLBB and GAO had in several steps bumped their estimates of FSLIC insolvency into the neighborhood of $70 billion. The American Bankers Association—a trade association for a class of competitors who might be stuck in the short run with a substantial portion of the costs of bailing out FSLIC—established a permanent FSLIC Oversight Committee in early 1988. In September 1988, this committee urged the formation of a reconstruction finance corporation for insolvent thrifts. It reported that its estimate of FSLIC's insolvency stood at $74 billion, but acknowledged that other credible estimates ran as high as $100 billion.

In the face of a massive economic insolvency in their insurance funds and lacking the political support to recapitalize their funds straightforwardly, the managers of decapitalized insurance funds adopted cosmetic policies that aggravated their funds' long-run problems. They extended the repertoire of accounting tricks available to regulators under GAAP to disguise further the magnitude of their current situation—tricks which required them to forbear from enforcing capital requirements for more than a small fraction of their decapitalized clients. It is interesting to compare my explanation with the thrift-industry perspective expressed by the retiring president of the U.S. League of Savings Associations, William O'Connell, in the preface to Strunk and Case (1988). He opines that "the deregulation of savings rates during a period of great inflation and high interest rates was the Achilles heel of the savings and loan business" (p. xiii) and that the FHLBB "was philosophically inclined to encourage institutions to undertake new kinds of investments that carried risks unfamiliar to them rather than exercising the greater regulatory responsibility it should have assumed in the light of these new risks" (p. xii). Although my analysis accepts and explains this philosophical inclination, I wish to stress that it is a dangerous mistake to believe that deposit-rate deregulation and expanded asset-holding powers brought zombie thrifts to their state of economic insolvency, or that they are helping to keep them there. Reversing these policies would not improve zombie firms' odds of becoming solvent again.

O'Connell asserts that it "is incredible that Congress undertook to deregulate savings rates during a period of extreme inflation, when interest rates had soared to double-digit levels" (p. xii). What I find incredible is that an industry leader can both: (1) presume zombie firms have a right to life more important than either taxpayers' right to responsible government or savers' rights to a fair return, and (2) deny what the 1970s taught us about how quickly ceilings on explicit deposit interest rates lose effectiveness over time. During 1966–80, deposit-rate ceilings became progressively less beneficial to thrift institutions. Disintermediation (i.e., depositor efforts to lend directly to corporate and government borrowers at markedly higher returns than they could earn by lending indirectly through banks and thrifts) and less-regulated competition from money-market mutual funds and credit unions increasingly squeezed thrift deposit flows. These forces also narrowed S&L profit margins by reinforcing bank and thrift efforts to attract additional deposits with implicit interest. Although it takes time for implicit deposit rates to catch up with surges in market interest rates, in financial markets as open as those of the modern era, one must expect implicit interest eventually to fill in nearly all the gap between the ceilings rate on explicit deposit interest and the free-market rate of deposit interest. Of course, with deposit-rate deregulation, the marketing strategies and branch-office networks adapted to paying implicit interest lost considerable value. This lost value clearly forms part of the industry's current profitability problem.

It is hard to argue against the likelihood that enhanced asset powers for thrifts offer opportunities to earn incremental profits. These incremental profits have two sources: on the cost side from potential scope economies (i.e., cost savings from spreading a broader product line across a given customer base) and on the revenue side from the benefits of being able both to diversify more freely and to make adaptations in explicit as well as implicit deposit interest rates. This enhanced profitability implied new possibilities for well-managed

S&Ls to rebuild their net worths. The rub is that the new powers also expanded opportunities for poorly managed thrifts to make fatal mistakes and for zombie firms to make go-for-broke gambles. To this extent, expanded powers and deposit-rate deregulation have contributed to many *individual* insolvencies.

But what initially brought so *many* S&Ls simultaneously into insolvency was the effect of the increasing trend in interest rates on what were predominantly short-funded portfolio positions. In turn, politically protected deposit-insurance subsidies had established incentives for thrifts to short-fund their mortgage lending and to maintain the resulting risk exposure even in the face of the rising interest rates observed in the 1960s and 1970s and short-term interest rates that often exceeded long-term interest rates. Deposit-insurance subsidies applied to other forms of under-regulated risks as well. Beginning in the mid-1960s, thrift managers increasingly recognized that accelerating inflation threatened their traditional earnings spreads. They saw that a strategy of continuing to short-fund their firms' mortgage holdings effectively placed a bet that interest rates would decline before authorities could or would force them to acknowledge the interim implicit losses these bets accrued whenever interest rates increased.

Expanding deposit-insurance coverage to $100,000 per account name in 1980 made deposit-insurance subsidies more accessible than ever to insolvent or aggressively growth-oriented thrifts. The resulting losses in the market value of their net assets, though still largely unrealized in an accounting sense, leave hundreds of these firms in a deep financial hole from which it is impossible to expect to extract themselves except by further risk taking.

Congress has underarmed top FSLIC officials and encouraged them to behave as one would expect western marshals to act in a Marx Brothers film. They and Congress have blindfolded themselves, worn their gunbelts around their ankles, and filled most chambers of their guns with blanks. They haphazardly supplied weapons and ammunition to a gang of hold-up men and in slapstick fashion helped most of the gang to escape frontier justice. Although lesser officials (examiners) dutifully continue to issue warrants for the perpetrators' arrest, the marshals have had neither the resources nor the will to shoot it out with more than a fraction of the zombie gang.

This metaphor clarifies the broad outlines of what needs to be done: give some entity (preferably a successor to the dishonored FSLIC) the resources to put every stubbornly unrecapitalizable member of the zombie-thrift gang in boot hill where they belong, and restructure the incentives facing politicians, regulators, and managers of insured thrifts to avoid a replay of this experience in the future. On what Washingtonians term the "Beltway range," the truly "discouraging word" is that it looks as if a great deal of further unpleasantness may have to unfold before this strategy becomes in *politicians'* career interests.

Note

1. This chapter draws extensively on Kane (1988a and b).

References

Barth, James R., and Michael G. Bradley. 1988. "Thrift Deregulation and Federal Deposit Insurance." Washington: Office of Policy and Economic Research, Federal Home Loan Bank Board. Paper prepared for Perspectives on Banking Regulation Conference, Federal Reserve Bank of Cleveland (November).
————, R. Dan Brumbaugh, Jr., and Daniel Sauerhaft. 1986. "Failure Costs of Government-Regulated Financial Firms: The Case of Thrift Institutions." Washington: Office of Policy and Economic Research, Federal Home Loan Bank Board (June).
Benston, George J., Robert A. Eisenbeis, Paul M. Horvitz, Edward J. Kane, and George G. Kaufman. 1986. *Perspectives on Safe and Sound Banking: Past, Present, and Future.* Cambridge, Mass.: MIT Press and the American Bankers Association.
Binstein, Michael. 1988. "Ed Gray: They Were Calling Me the Gestapo." *Regardie's Magazine* (October), pp. 91–96.
Black, Fisher, Merton Miller, and Richard Posner. 1978. "An Approach to the Regulation of Bank Holding Companies." *Journal of Business* 51 (July), pp. 379–411.
Buser, Stephen A., Andrew H. Chen, and Edward J. Kane. 1981. "Federal Deposit Insurance, Regulatory Policy, and Optimal Bank Capital." *Journal of Finance* 36 (March), pp. 51–60.
Campbell, Tim S., and Anthony M. Marino. 1988. "On the Incentives for Managers to Make Myopic Investment Decisions." Los Angeles: University of Southern California. Unpublished manuscript.

Carron, Andrew S. 1983. *The Rescue of the Thrift Industry*. Studies in the Regulation of Economic Activity. Washington: The Brookings Institution.

——. 1988. "The Thrift Industry Crisis of the 1980s: What Went Wrong." Paper prepared for The Future of the Thrift Industry. Fourteenth Annual Conference of the Federal Home Loan Bank Board of San Francisco.

Garcia, Gillian. 1988. "A New Link in the Chain: A Comment." Washington: General Accounting Office (unpublished).

Guttentag, Jack and Richard Herring. 1982. "Insolvency of Financial Institutions: Assessment and Regulatory Disposition," in Paul Wachtel, ed. *Crisis in the Economic and Financial Structure*. Lexington, Mass.: Lexington Books, pp. 99–126.

Kane, Edward J. 1981. "Reregulation, Savings and Loan Diversification, and the Flow of Housing Finance," in *Savings and Loan Asset Management Under Deregulation*. San Francisco: Federal Home Loan Bank of San Francisco, pp. 81–109.

——. 1985. *The Gathering Crisis in Federal Deposit Insurance*. Cambridge, Mass: MIT Press.

——. 1987. "Dangers of Capital Forbearance: The Case of the FSLIC and Zombie S&Ls." *Contemporary Policy Issues*, 5 (Jan.), pp. 77–83.

——. 1988a. "Changing Incentives Facing Financial-Services Regulators." Manuscript prepared for a Conference at the Federal Reserve Bank of Cleveland, forthcoming in *Journal of Financial Services Research* 3(2).

——. 1988b. "The Looting of FSLIC: What Went Wrong?" Panel discussion prepared for the Fourteenth Annual Conference of the Federal Home Loan Bank of San Francisco (December 8).

Kareken, John H. 1983. "Deposit Insurance Reform or Deregulation Is the Cart Not the Horse." *Quarterly Review*. Federal Reserve Bank of Minneapolis (Spring), pp. 1–9.

——, and Neil Wallace. 1978. "Deposit Insurance and Bank Regulation: A Partial Equilibrium Exposition." *Journal of Business* (July).

McCulloch, J. Huston. 1981. "Interest Rate Risk and Capital Adequacy for Traditional Banks and Financial Intermediaries," in Sherman Maisel, ed. *Risk and Capital Adequacy in Commercial Banks*. Chicago: University of Chicago Press for the National Bureau of Economic Research, pp. 223–248.

Meltzer, Allan H. 1967. "Major Issues in the Regulation of Financial Institutions." *Journal of Political Economy, Supplement* 75 (August), pp. 482–501.

Merton, Robert C. 1978. "On the Cost of Deposit Insurance When There Are Surveillance Costs." *Journal of Business* 51 (July), pp. 439–452.

Myers, Stewart C., and Nicholas Majluf. 1984. "Corporate Financing and Investment Decisions When Firms Have Information that Investors

Do Not Have." *Journal of Financial Economics* 13 (June), pp. 187–221.

Narayanan, M.P. 1985. "Managerial Incentives for Short-Term Results." *Journal of Finance* 40 (December), pp. 1469–84.

Pyle, David H. 1983. "Pricing Deposit Insurance: The Effects of Mismeasurement." Federal Reserve Bank of San Francisco and University of California, Berkeley (October).

Scott, Kenneth W., and Thomas Mayer. 1971. "Risk and Regulation in Banking: Some Proposals for Deposit Insurance." *Stanford Law Review* 23 (May), pp. 857–902.

Strunk, Norman, and Fred Case. 1988. *Where Deregulation Went Wrong: A Look at the Causes Behind Savings and Loan Failures in the 1980s.* Washington: U.S. League of Savings Institutions.

Wang, George H.K., Daniel Sauerhaft, and Donald Edwards. 1987. "Predicting Thrift-Institution Examination Ratings." Working Paper No. 131. Washington: Office of Policy and Economic Research, Federal Home Loan Bank Board (June).

AN ALGEBRAIC SUMMARY OF THE ARGUMENT

This book portrays policies of covering up and not explicitly financing FSLIC's implicit losses as a type of "gambling" by politicians and regulators that is encouraged by a critical defect in the budget discipline under which the federal government operates. This defect consists of focusing budget discipline entirely on the flow of explicit receipts and expenditures over the next fiscal year, while ignoring the impact of equally important implicit receipts and expenditures that are inherent in movements in the values of federal commitments and guarantees. In this appendix, the argument is restated to put into symbolic terms the major effects of the kind of gambles that federal officials have made and to explain officials' disposition to making negative-present-value gambles as behavior that is rational because of principal-agent conflicts.

LOOKING AT FSLIC AS A GOVERNMENT-CONTROLLED CORPORATION

One of the most closely studied principal-agent relationships occurs between a corporation's stockholders and managers. It is generally agreed that stockholders must worry about the possibility that managers will sometimes pursue their own interests at the expense of those of their corporation's stockholders. As a *government-controlled* corporation, FSLIC is essentially a corporate subsidiary of a higher-order corporation or "holding company" that we call the federal government. In this conception, FSLIC is a corporate enterprise that is run by two layers of managers: FSLIC and FHLBB bureaucrats and the elected federal politicians to which these lesser officials ultimately report. In turn, the federal government is seen as a corporation whose stockholders constitute the taxpaying citizenry. To apply corporate finance concepts to a government-controlled corporation, one must recognize the existence of implicit assets, implicit liabilities, and implicit capital. These implicit sources of value trace to *de facto* costs and revenues inherent in the operation of a government enterprise that are not formally acknowledged by conventional accounting schemes. On the liability side, a government connection imposes a loose implicit obligation on a corporation's managers to lessen conflicts between the broad public interest and the narrower corporate interests of the enterprise for which they are specifically responsible. Correspondingly, a government connection gives a corporation's managers and the corporation's debtholders a conjectural right to expect some degree of financial support from the government to flow to the corporation in the event it runs into trouble.

Whether or not one calls FSLIC economically insolvent turns critically on how one treats the value of the implicit and conjectural guarantees that FSLIC obligations receive from the U.S. Treasury. Depositors at FSLIC-insured institutions currently act as if they regard what is well publicized as a $100-to-$150 billion hole in FSLIC's explicit balance sheet to be reliably filled in by the value of the *de facto* or implicit guarantees that the federal government accords to FSLIC. However, the conjectural nature of these guarantees creates uncertainty that encourages the public to test repeatedly the reliability of a troubled insurer's government support. Repeated testing of a capital-short deposit-insurance fund raises its cost of operation and creates opportunities for political or bureaucratic misplays that could trigger a fund meltdown.

VALUING A DEPOSIT-INSURANCE ENTERPRISE

As sporadic efforts to privatize government assets indicate, even a government-controlled corporation may, in principle, be said to have a well-defined market value, MV. This value may be conceived as the price that a well-informed and willing private party would pay to take over or buy out the government's stake in the enterprise. Although not directly observable, this value constitutes a "pseudo" aggregate stock price that may, in principle, be calculated as the net present value of the future cash flows the corporation's operations generate.

FSLIC's annual deposit-insurance revenues come from two sources: explicit insurance premiums (P) and investment earnings on insurance reserves. Earnings on reserves may be conceived to be the product of an average portfolio return (r) and the size of the insurer's fund of reserves (R). Deposit-insurance costs consist of monitoring costs (C_M) and losses incurred in resolving client insolvencies (C_L). In any year, the flow of net revenue to the insurer (F) could be expressed as the difference between the two revenue and cost flows. Schematically, we may write this sum as follows:

> Premium Income (P)
> + Investment Earnings (rR)
> − Monitoring Costs (C_M)
> − Losses Incurred in Resolving Client Insolvencies (C_L)
> ——————————————————————————
> FSLIC Net Revenue (F)

Algebraically, we may express the ideas embodied in this schematic as an equation:

$$F = P + rR - C_M - C_L. \tag{4.1}$$

To calculate the present value of a stream of projected future net revenues, we need to discount the series of projected future cash flows by the insurer's cost of capital (r_I). The discounting process is greatly simplified if for convenience we assume that FSLIC's projected future flows of net revenue are anticipated to go on forever and can be satisfactorily approximated as occurring at an unchanging average or "permanent" amount F each year. These assumptions allow us to model FSLIC's stream of future cash flows as if it were a perpetuity. As a perpetuity, the true market value or pseudo-stock price of FSLIC's insurance enterprise would be:

$$MV_I = 1/r_I [P + rR - C_M - C_L] \tag{4.2}$$

For FSLIC's insurance enterprise to be economically insolvent, the market value given in (4.2) must be negative. This means that the government would have to pay a private party to take over financial responsibility for FSLIC's affairs. It also means that the permanent value of its annualized cash flow is projected to be negative.

For an economically insolvent enterprise to stay in operation, its net losses must be financed in some way. When an insolvency first begins to emerge, losses are often disguised as a temporary phenomenon and financed by some combination of selling off and borrowing against a firm's net assets. This is essentially the path of adjustment FSLIC has followed in recent years.

However, such adjustments leave an insolvent firm increasingly less liquid and make the permanence of its insolvency more and

more difficult to hide from outsiders. Eventually, the enterprise becomes unable to service its debt on its own. To cure its insolvency,
the firm must either be liquidated or be restructured as at least a
breakeven enterprise.

Whenever a separately incorporated subsidiary is revealed to be
economically insolvent, the officers of the firm's parent corporation
have a legal right to stiff the subsidiary's creditors. By invoking the
principle of limited liability, the top officials of FSLIC's holding
company (i.e., elected federal politicians) have an option to disavow
the implicit and explicit net losses accumulated by a separately incorporated subsidiary such as FSLIC. In the ordinary business world,
this is done by being willing to permit the subsidiary to go into
liquidation.

Even in the private sector, holding companies whose officers decide to walk away from an insolvency in one of their subsidiaries
are treated to some degree as financial weasels who have disowned
a moral obligation. As a result, firms that show themselves willing
to play such financial hardball usually suffer a decline in credit
standing. This knowledge leads a subsidiary's debtholders always to
conjecture that the parent will use its own corporate resources to
make good at least some of a subsidiary's losses.

In the case of a government-controlled corporation, the fallout from
walking away from a subsidiary's debt is political as well as economic. If FSLIC were to be liquidated, FSLIC's angry debtholders
would organize to punish the government officials that burned them
by unleashing various forms of political vitriol. FSLIC's debtholders'
substantial capacity to hurt them has to weigh heavily on the politicians who must ultimately decide whether to make good on implicit
obligations and explicit promises to support FSLIC's finances with
Treasury resources. Besides the fact of federal ownership, in a FSLIC
meltdown FSLIC creditors' logical case and the justifiability of their
anger would be strengthened by the knowledge that in 1982 and
1987 joint congressional resolutions declared it to be the "sense of
Congress" that the full faith and credit of the U.S. government stands
behind the obligations of all federal deposit-insurance subsidiaries.

When the concentrated economic interest of a limited number of
citizens collides in a perceived crisis situation with the diffuse interests of taxpayers in general, the concentrated interest almost always wins. Because its members are better informed and have
dramatically more at stake than ordinary taxpayers, it pays them—
whereas it does not pay ordinary taxpayers—to incur the costs of

developing and exercising a high level of political influence on the outcome.

IMPLICATIONS FOR OPTIMALLY MANAGING
FSLIC CASH FLOWS

This political analysis leads one to assume that taxpayers' liability for losses rung up by FSLIC is effectively an unlimited one. Before informed taxpayers would accept such an obligation, they would have to be convinced of two points. First, the nonpecuniary benefits society receives from FSLIC would have to be sufficient to cover FSLIC's losses. Second, for a given level of social benefits, FSLIC's managers would have to be seen as minimizing the capitalized value of the firm's strictly pecuniary losses laid out in equation (4.2).

From this perspective, almost all the actions authorities have taken in recent years to minimize explicit accounting measures of FSLIC's losses and capital shortfall represent exercises in false economy. Covering up the agency's implicit losses has increased the long-run costs of adequately refinancing FSLIC in two principal ways. First, FSLIC and FSLIC-insured institutions have had to finance taxpayer-guaranteed explicit debt at explicit plus implicit interest rates that average 50-to-100 basis points over Treasury interest rates. Second, understating FSLIC's cumulative shortage has reduced political pressure for making timely corrections of well-known weaknesses in the deposit-insurance system. These continuing weaknesses are responsible for saddling FSLIC with additional implicit losses almost every day.

Clearly, the value of each variable on the righthand side of equation (4.2) is conditioned simultaneously on the bureau's procedures, policies, and political constraints, and on the net worth and risk exposure of the client firms it guarantees. In particular, the permanent value of losses incurred in resolving client insolvencies (C_L) may be said to rise with volatility in the financial environment (V), with the risk exposure of the fund's clients (E_R), and with clients' capacity to conceal the consequence of their risk taking from the agency's monitors (C_C) and to fall with the amount and quality of FSLIC's own monitoring efforts and insolvency-resolution activity (A). If we assume (for the sake of argument) that FSLIC monitoring efforts are always technically efficient, we may bundle these sign restrictions

Table A-4-1 UNCONTROLLED, PARTIALLY CONTROLLED, AND
CONTROL VARIABLES AFFECTING THE VALUE OF
FSLIC'S PSEUDO-STOCK PRICE

Completely Exogenous Variables	Indirectly Controlled Variables	Potential Controls
r	R	P
V	C_L	C_M
	E_R	A
	C_C	

into an equation that has the following partially defined functional
form:

$$C_L = C_L(\overset{(+)}{V}, \overset{(+)}{E_R}, \overset{(+)}{C_C}, \overset{(-)}{C_M}, \overset{(-)}{A}). \tag{4.3}$$

In (4.3), the parenthetical signs express the qualitative impact that
each argument of the function has on the value of C_L.

If we treat the value of FSLIC's nonpecuniary social services as
fixed, taxpayers would want FSLIC officials to maximize the enterprise's market value or pseudo-stock price (4.2). To make this as-
signment operational, we may substitute (4.3) into (4.2) and consider
which variables are given and which ones are at least potentially
under FSLIC control. Table A-4-1 divides the variables into three
categories:

1. Those that are virtually exogenous (the interest rate, r, and the
   volatility of the economic environment, V);
2. Those that are indirectly or partially controlled, in the sense
   that their projected future value varies noticeably as FSLIC ad-
   justs its premiums, monitoring effort, or insolvency-resolution
   activity: R, C_L, E_R, and C_C; and
3. FSLIC's potential control variables (its premium, P; its monitoring effort, C_M; and its insolvency-resolution activity, A).

If no conflicts of interest existed among FSLIC's managers, elected
politicians, and federal taxpayers, premiums, monitoring, and insolvency-resolution effort would be set at the values that would
maximize (4.2), which would be the course of action preferred by
taxpayers if they were fully informed.

Chapter Five

EVIDENCE OF REGULATORY GAMBLING: THE MELTDOWNS OF TWO DEPOSIT-INSURANCE FUNDS

Previous chapters document the decline of FSLIC's financial condition over time and explain the policy mistakes that led to this decline. This chapter supports and extends this analysis in two ways. First, to round out the picture of what can happen when a deposit-insurance fund becomes economically decapitalized, I discuss how a longstanding condition of deposit-insurer weakness may accelerate into a full-fledged meltdown and outline the sequence of events that complete and incomplete meltdowns entail. Second, I summarize legal and government documents that provide clear evidence of regulatory gambling by the top administrators of deposit-insurance funds that failed in Ohio and Maryland.

WHERE TO LOOK FOR EMPIRICAL EVIDENCE FOR OR AGAINST THE INCENTIVE-BREAKDOWN HYPOTHESIS

The discussion in chapter four focuses on the self-interest of politicians and an insurance fund's top managers. It maintains that, when a deposit-insurance fund becomes deeply insolvent, authorities are tempted to cover up adverse information about fund performance and to gamble alongside their zombie clients on schemes that have only a low probability of overcoming their implicit or *de facto* losses.

The theory predicts that, in the early stages of an insurance fund's substantial *de facto* insolvency, politicians may not want to deal with the problem and top regulators may become more concerned about leaving government service with an untroubled record than with minimizing additional and unobservable implicit losses that the fund might develop on their watch. The issue is whether public servants ever succumb to the temptation to put personal concerns ahead of their duty to the citizenry at large.

Economic analysis is built on the presumption that people perceive incentives and respond to them in terms of their enlightened self-interest. Opportunities for "moral enlightenment" open the possibility that sainted public servants may exist, who condition their self-esteem primarily on how well their actions serve completely altruistic ends. But thoroughly altruistic conditioning seems rare in human history—so rare that it is hard to take seriously alleged readings of subjective experience that treat the overarching altruism of public officials as a given.

Psychologists tell us that the need of individuals to minimize cognitive dissonance (i.e., inconsistent psychological motivations) could lead politicians and deposit-institution regulators to misread their own motives. By the same token, if consciously self-interested behavior were dominant, it is doubtful that informal or even scientific surveys of individual government decisionmakers could document its extent. Survey respondents would have little motivation to confess what others might interpret as quasi-shameful or perhaps even criminal lapses in behavior.

A more promising population of subjects to survey could be constructed from lobbyists of various kinds. Such a survey would seek to measure whether and how regulated firms and their trade associations *believe* they actually influence regulatory policies. In particular, a survey researcher could seek to compile these parties' estimates of how effective it is on average to discuss with individual regulators and politicians how their own future government careers and postgovernment employment prospects might be affected by pushing for or against tough regulatory decisions. The researcher would also do well to measure when, where, and how frequently such potentially meaningful exchanges of view might take place and to note that cognitive dissonance may lead these subjects to exaggerate the influence they wield.

Alternatively, one can look for admissions of conflicted regulatory behavior in legal proceedings and legislative hearings. The question is whether officials were either aware, or culpably ignorant in their lack of awareness, of the disastrous long-run consequences of following policies of coverup and forbearance. In investigative forums, regulators can be pressed by the weight of collateral evidence and by penalties that can be imposed for making false statements to give damaging testimony against themselves. For this reason, such testimonial evidence provides a particularly promising opportunity for testing the incentive-breakdown hypothesis.

THE SIX STAGES OF A DEPOSIT-INSURANCE MELTDOWN

To gain perspective on what Ohio and Maryland regulators have testified about their deposit-insurance funds' breakdowns, it is necessary to understand the background of information and events against which these regulators' decisions took place. We intend to organize this background information to show that a complete deposit-insurance meltdown passes through six stages. An incomplete or uncompleted meltdown such as FSLIC has experienced skips the open bureaucratic-breakdown stage (stage three), but may pass through all or most of the other stages.

Stage One. A necessary but not sufficient condition for a fund meltdown is a shortage of explicit reserves. Such a shortage does not develop overnight. This means that the first stage of a meltdown is a string of client losses large enough to exhaust the fund's explicit resources if these losses were recognized hypothetically and made good by the fund. The length of this *loss-generation stage* is extended by blockages in the flow of information, both about the size of imbedded losses and ongoing client risk taking and about the impact of these losses and risks on the market value of the net worth of the insurance fund. Client managers instinctively try to conceal serious losses from examiners representing the fund and from their accountants, stockholders, customers, and competitors. The different classes of state and federal regulators that oversee an institution routinely share with each other only part of any unfavorable information that may come into their possession, and share almost none of this information with depositors, stockholders, and other clients of the insurance fund. In part this reflects authorities' propensity to reject or deny the unpleasant implications of a client's unbooked losses when unfavorable evidence first comes to their attention. It also reflects a fear of being blamed for initiating or aggravating depositor runs or unfavorable movements in the price of a troubled firm's stock. But once a client comes under actual customer pressure, a habit of routinely not sharing information flows can easily deteriorate into acts of coverup.

The depth of the shortage a fund ultimately develops has three interacting causes: (1) regulatory failure; (2) speculation, concealment, and in some cases fraud at client institutions; and (3) customers' faith that somehow politicians will eventually appropriate resources to rescue the fund.

As the stage of loss generation becomes prolonged, concern dawns among depositors about the repayment capacity of the fund's highest-flying clients and of the fund itself. This dawning tends to occur first among sophisticated customers who appreciate the possibility that a potentially costly meltdown could occur. For formally insured depositors, potential costs consist of the possibilities that their withdrawal rights might be limited or their deposit interest rates on term accounts rolled back to below-market levels. These concerns put questionable client firms into a condition that may be called a slow or "silent" run.

In a full-fledged run, a large number of an institution's depositors line up electronically and at teller windows to sweep their deposits into a safer repository. In a silent run, only a relatively small fraction of depositors threatens to withdraw funds. Depositor confidence is wavering but has not yet collapsed all together. The opportunity cost of closing an established deposit relationship makes customers willing to live with their growing doubts as long as they are adequately compensated for doing so. The downward pressure that declining customer confidence generates on an institution's net flow of new deposits may be overcome by paying higher deposit interest rates or expanding the use of nondeposit (especially collateralized or asset-backed) sources of funds. This possibility makes it inappropriate to presume that a silent run entails either a loss of deposits or even a shrinkage in an institution's rate of asset growth. To analyze fluctuations in depositor confidence in a deposit-insurance fund, it is necessary to draw simultaneously on evidence concerning deposit flows, deposit interest rates, and the growth of nondeposit debt.

By themselves, for example, the interest-rate differentials between thrift certificate of deposit rates and Treasury yields (discussed in chapter three) suggest a waxing and waning of depositor concerns about the repayment capacities of FSLIC and GAAP-insolvent thrifts. However, the waning of concern in late-1988 these data suggest does not reflect the true situation. Introducing data on net deposit flows would show important adjustments were also occurring in the nature of thrift funding. In late 1988 and early 1989, a net deposit outflow has been tolerated and certificates of deposits issued by desperate institutions have in many cases been marketed to other thrifts for below-market placement fees by Federal Home Loan Banks energetically acting as agents.

Stage Two. Authorities see themselves as dutybound to prevent a fund's shortage of explicit reserves from deteriorating into a widespread loss of customer confidence. When bad news about individual institutions triggers even a rationally based silent run, they worry about the possibility that this run may spread to other institutions and in the worst case undermine customer confidence in the deposit-insurance fund that supports them.

The second stage of a meltdown occurs when silent runs become endemic. This condition may be described as the stage of *repeated testing* of fund resources and backup political support. During this stage, authorities' ability to contain crises at individual institutions and identifiable blocks of institutions is tested severely.

To resolve growing doubt about willingness and ability of the institution to live up to its obligations, depositors must evaluate the financial resources and integrity of the guarantor. Whenever a possibility exists that the guarantor may not fully discharge its liabilities, depositors must look into the identity and strength of whatever parties effectively guarantee the guarantor. The backup guarantors for federal deposit insurance are parties on whom regulators and legislators may be expected in a crisis to dump the financial burden of financing an insurance bureau's shortfall. These potential ratepayers may be grouped into three tiers: (1) the stronger members of the pool of institutions directly covered by the troubled fund; (2) other close competitors of institutions in this pool, whom authorities may presume to derive some potentially taxable benefit from the associated exit of troubled firms from the market; and (3) the general taxpayer.

The more reasonable it seems to doubt whether deposit insurers can service their contingent obligations from their own resources, the more reasonable it becomes to worry about how smoothly and effectively the political system could distribute the burden of recapitalizing them across the three tiers of back-up guarantors. When insolvencies in state-sponsored deposit-insurance corporations in Mississippi, Nebraska, Ohio, and Maryland revealed themselves in recent years, settlement of their outstanding liabilities was noticeably delayed as backup guarantors who professed to be surprised by their plight actively resisted legislative efforts to levy a share of the liability shortfall on them.

Without a deep pocket into which to cram losses more or less as they occur, maintenance of public confidence in the insurance funds depends on maintaining public confidence that regulators and elected officials can deal with emerging problems in a roughly optimal manner. This means making pronouncements that indicate that authorities understand the size of the problem at least as well as worried depositors do and confirming authorities' willingness to make good on deposit-insurance promises. As mere human beings, government officials cannot prove equal to every task the economy puts before them. Hence, in any period in which the insurance agencies have become decapitalized, officials may not succeed in maintaining public confidence. In this stage, the system could break down anytime.

Stage Three. Inadequate risk-management systems and the absence of explicit arrangements for funding the pledge of government faith and credit that is perceived to back the insurance funds open up the possibility of *open bureaucratic breakdown*. Recent deposit-insurance crises in Ohio and Maryland demonstrate that a volatile and competitive financial environment can provide elected officials opportunities for dangerously misplaying a developing crisis.

In these states, the well-publicized death throes of one or more large clients were allowed to amplify longstanding conditions of silent runs into a full-fledged loss of confidence. In a complete meltdown, officials prove unwilling to promise sufficient resources to re-establish the deposit-insurance corporation's credibility. This leads to an open meltdown of the supporting deposit-insurance fund and to panic runs at other questionable clients of the deposit-insurance scheme.

The Ohio deposit-insurance crisis even shook financial markets outside of Ohio, not because of the size of the insolvency, but because Ohio and federal politicians surprised capital-market participants by trying to weasel out of what the market conjectured to be their responsibility for backing up the resources of the Ohio Deposit Guarantee Fund (ODGF) (Kane 1988). The temporary unwillingness of Ohio authorities to make good the losses suffered by ODGF amounted to their stopping to assess the relative willingness of Ohio taxpayers and federal authorities to underwrite the costs of making good the losses that might otherwise be visited on ODGF-insured depositors. In calling a prolonged banking holiday for ODGF institutions instead of promptly promising to recapitalize the guarantee fund, Ohio's Democratic governor challenged the Republican-controlled Ohio legislature and federal regulators and politicians to a multisided game of chicken. Playing out this game confirmed market participants' longstanding presumption that in a political showdown the concentrated interests of depositors in troubled institutions tend eventually to overcome the diffuse interests of the various taxpayers that the U.S. financial system makes into risk-bearers of last resort. The spectacular and corrupt failure of a securities firm (ESM Securities in the case of the ODGF and Bevil, Bresler, & Schulman in the Maryland case) and the imprudently large exposure of one or more large client thrifts to a single such credit were the proximate causes of both funds' demise. However, the ultimate cause was the false security that extensive deposit-insurer guarantees gave both to depositors in insolvent clients and to other insured firms. Although chartered by special legislation as allegedly "private" corporations, the insurers' official-looking seals and corporate names were widely mistaken as evidence of formal state backing. As unrealized losses at insured institutions grew increasingly larger than fund reserves, this security became more and more illusory because it placed a correspondingly greater burden on fund managers and state regulators to oversee insured institutions skillfully.

Common sense holds that it is not sensible to depend on others (particularly agents such as politicians and bureaucrats) always to act sensibly. For example, as drivers, all of us soon learn that depending on other drivers to behave optimally is a sure formula for eventually bringing on a serious crash.

Deposit-insurance incentives sorely and perversely test the moral and financial integrity of managers of decapitalized deposit institutions and decapitalized insurance funds. No guarantee scheme can endure forever whose information, monitoring, and enforcement subsystems put the interests of taxpayers, politicians, regulators, and deposit-institution executives deeply into conflict.

Stage Four. The fourth stage is the *recapitalization* or *bailout stage.* Stage three can be avoided if authorities tire of market testing soon enough to recapitalize the insurance fund before someone misplays a pressure situation. But whether or not an open meltdown occurs, testing will not stop until authorities work out the terms and extent of the government assistance that they are prepared to offer to lessen the hole in the insurer's explicit finances. This means telling taxpayers how big the deposit-insurance bill has become, which particular groups of taxpayers are going to be asked to pay this bill, and how long the payments will last.

In the absence of an open meltdown, however, political infighting tends to work against full recapitalization, keeping insurer resources too small to make silent runs completely irrational. Such inadequate capitalizations may be exemplified by the Competitive Equality Banking Act of 1987. This act expanded FSLIC's borrowing authority and included a second joint congressional resolution stating a "sense of Congress" guarantee of the federal deposit insurers. But on a market-value basis, it put very little additional explicit net worth into

FSLIC's balance sheet. Inadequate recapitalizations are best conceived as variations of stage four that trigger stages five and six without moving authorities completely out of the testing stage two.

Stage Five. Recapitalization seeks to provide to whatever entity might take over an insolvent fund's equity stake in client firms the resources to sort out efficiently which clients should and should not be permitted to survive. This sorting-out process may be called the *triage stage*. The name triage originates in medical usage. It refers to the process by which doctors in a battlefield or disaster situation decide which of a number of casualties awaiting emergency treatment should in fact be treated and in what order. Triage seeks to allocate a fixed bundle of medical resources across a set of casualties according to their potential for ultimate recovery and the extent and immediacy of their need for medical care.

The analogue to medical care for insolvent thrifts is adequate recapitalization. Delaying recapitalization of zombie thrifts delays and distorts triage, generating incremental financial and political costs and benefits. Available evidence indicates that continually delaying the treatment of widespread insolvency problems over long periods of time is bound to increase the amount of insolvency that must ultimately be resolved (Barth, Brumbaugh, Sauerhaft, and Wang 1986; Kane 1987).

Triage is urgently required for almost all thrifts whose intangible net worth is negative (table 3-3) and for a number of additional thrifts whose tangible net worth remains very small. It is by no means enough to recapitalize only FSLIC's equity stake in the worst few hundred of the roughly 800 to 1,000 zombie and near-zombie firms in existence. While this will provide some temporary relief, the firms exempted from treatment will continue to face distorted incentives. And the go-for-broke strategies to which they will be attracted will add billions of additional dollars to FSLIC's final bill.

Stage Six. The final stage in a deposit-insurance meltdown may be called the *blame-redistribution stage*. It is played out over a long period of time in the courts, in legislative hearings, and in the press.

Blame redistribution has financial, political, and criminal dimensions. It consists of formal and informal efforts both to pin responsibility for the fund's losses on a set of specific scapegoats and to force formal restitution from managers, accountants, and lawyers whose pursuit of deposit-insurance subsidies may have overstepped legal boundaries.

In state and federal courts, regulators bring civil suits seeking damages from accounting firms for allegedly issuing improperly "clean" audit reports for failing firms. Regulators also initiate numerous civil and criminal actions against managers and lawyers for failing firms, accusing them of engaging in various questionable acts.

At the legislative level, hearings and detailed investigations are held to clarify the facts and to assign official blame. But politicians and regulators seldom focus on what transforms pre-existing deposit-insurance weaknesses into a full-fledged crisis. This is not the insolvency of a particular set of clients. It is the absence of reliable and comprehensive information on the condition of other insured S&Ls and authorities' reluctance to enunciate in timely fashion a credible policy for resolving the fallout of insurer insolvency that is bound to develop in the wake of closing seriously insolvent firms.

EVIDENCE OF REGULATORY GAMBLING IN OHIO AND MARYLAND[1]

Legislative hearings and reports, sworn depositions, and testimony in court paint a clear picture of regulatory gambling prior to the meltdown of the Ohio and Maryland deposit-insurance funds.

The Ohio Case

The proximate cause of ODGF's meltdown was a persistent depositor run on its largest (and politically most influential) client, the deeply insolvent Home State Savings. The bulk of Home State's accumulated $150 million capital shortage came from overcollateralized reverse repurchase agreements on which the counterparty (ESM Securities of Fort Lauderdale, Florida) defaulted.

Digression on Repurchase Agreements. To appreciate how Home State's shortage developed, it is necessary to understand the obligations accepted by parties to a repurchase agreement. Such an agreement is called a "repo" in the trade. A repo is a contract that resembles a collateralized loan. It specifies two mirror-image transactions that are separated in time. The first transaction is to be executed immediately and is said to take place in the "spot" or "cash" market. The second transaction amounts to a mutual obligation to reverse the first transaction on an agreed upon future date at a price that embodies a fixed rate of accrued interest. This obligation to repurchase or resell is called a "forward" contract.

In the spot market, one signatory can be construed as making a loan of cash that the borrower or "counterparty" collateralizes with an equally valuable collection of securities. In the language of accountants, the cash lender debits cash and credits an equal amount of securities; the cash borrower credits cash and debits securities.

The term "repurchase" refers to the forward part of the contract and is used to clarify that formal title to the specific securities which constitute the collateral for the loan actually passes to the cash lender. Title to the securities passes back to the other counterparty (i.e., the cash borrower) when the forward contract is executed by repayment of the cash loan.

In many cases, the securities themselves move along with the title. In such instances, during the interim the temporary owner is responsible for their safety. Although the party "minding" the securities receives a formal right to resell them to a third party before the repurchase date, it is obliged to substitute equivalent capital whenever it does so.

The term "reverse repurchase agreement" is used to describe the cash borrower's side of the contract. This party may be construed as raising cash funds by lending securities to the contract's counterparty, who is obliged to return the securities for the specified amount of cash at the forward date. An institution executing a reverse repo sells securities for cash and agrees to buy these same securities back at a fixed rate of accrued interest on the agreed-upon future date. The obligation to buy back the securities may be secured by putting up securities whose value as collateral exceeds the repurchase obligation. For Home State, table 5-1 shows that such agreements (listed under "other borrowed money") served as an increasingly important source of apparently low interest-rate funds. Table 5-2 shows that Home State's deposit interest costs were relatively high.

Regulatory Gambling. ESM's fraud consisted of reselling Home State's collateral without bothering to replace it with equivalent securities. When each successive agreement matured, ESM simply borrowed Home State's now phantom securities (which ESM falsely warranted to be stored in its vaults) all over again. Proceeds from reselling Home State's securities to third parties were used to cover ESM's losses in other ventures and to pay the salaries of ESM personnel.

Evidence of other fraudulent activity at ESM had been uncovered by the Office of the U.S. Comptroller of the Currency in 1976 and by the Federal Home Loan Bank of Chicago in 1981. These regulators had ordered their regulatees to abstain from transactions with ESM.

Tables 5-1 to 5-3 summarize some of the unsettling information top Ohio regulators received during the five years preceding Home State's failure.

Data in table 5-1 indicate that losses imbedded in Home State's scheduled items and securities portfolio exceeded the accounting value of its net worth from at least June 30, 1981 forward. Table 5-2 shows that, even when ceiling rates at FSLIC-insured thrifts were relaxed, Home State continued to pay differentially higher rates of deposit interest. Firms that pay above-average interest rates for deposits must be presumed to be taking above-average risks. The addendum to table 5-1, which characterizes Home State's over-collateralized reverse-repo position with ESM as a "time-bomb," establishes that examiners recognized the dangers to ODGF raised by Home State's manner of operation and were disturbed by higher officials' inappropriate lack of concern. Table 5-3 clarifies that the pattern of inadequate regulatory discipline persisted over several years.

In deposition testimony about how they could have permitted Home State to maintain and expand its concentration of risky business with a questionable firm, former top regulators repeatedly expressed the view that to help Home State grow out of its problems appeared to them—although it did not so appear to their examination staffs—as the only reasonable course of action. These officials apparently feared depositor runs more than they feared the incentives that led an insolvent firm to roll the dice in ways that imposed further losses on the ODGF.

However, their appreciation of how bad Home State's attempts to grow out of its problems were proceeding appeared to grow over their term in office. Although accounting data available to these regulators were not sufficient to tell them about ESM's fraudulent use of Home State's collateral, information on file at the ODSL (shown in tables 5-1 and 5-2) was sufficient to establish that interest-rate increases had made Home State an economically insolvent firm. It was clear to ODSL examiners that the reverse repos had a non-negligible risk of default. They saw Home State as pursuing a high-risk strategy for curing its insolvency at the risk of bankrupting its supporting deposit-insurance fund.

The visible part of Home State's insolvency parallels the initial wave of decapitalization at FSLIC-insured thrifts. As highly leveraged long lenders and short borrowers, many thrifts found that the run-up in interest rates observed during 1965–82 wiped out the economic value of enterprise-contributed capital. For years, the viability of these firms depended entirely on the credibility of deposit-

Table 5-1 REPORTED SIZE OF HOME STATE SAVINGS, AT SELECTED DATES DURING 1979–85 ($ million)

Date	Total Assets	Scheduled Items	Net Worth	Imbedded Losses on Selected Gov. and Agency Securities	Other Borrowed Money
6/30/79	286.0		11.7		65.1[a]
12/31/79	279.0	5.2	12.5		39.8
6/30/80	535.1	17.1	13.0		232.4
12/31/80	548.1	7.0	13.7		209.5
6/30/81	579.3	11.5	14.2	22.1	198.5
12/31/81	617.7	10.3	13.1		148.3
6/30/82	560.2	12.9	11.9	31.1	83.8
12/31/82	562.1	14.1	16.3		86.0
6/30/83	1,101.2	19.6	17.0		607.3
9/30/83	1,146.2		16.3	46.5 (some hedging)	614.9
12/31/83	1,146.9		15.8		610.0
3/31/84	1,148.4		16.2		589.0
6/30/84	1,101.2		17.2		561.2
9/30/84	1,420.2		20.1		755.3
12/31/84	1,438.0		19.7		713.2
2/23/85	1,424.5		20.5		685.7
4/30/85	626.0		6.2		

Source: 1979 through 6/30/83 figures and imbedded losses for 9/30/83 taken from ODSL examination reports, given in Appendix to testimony given by Sylvester Hentschel to the Ohio Joint Select Committee (OJSC) on Savings and Loans of the 116th Ohio General Assembly. Later figures comes from Monthly Reports filed with the Ohio Division of Savings and Loans (ODSL).

Note: The statutory net worth requirement was 3 percent either of current deposits or of the 5-year average of deposits.

a. This amount is in excess of allowable "additional borrowing" under regulations in effect at this time.

Addendum to Table 5-1

Ticking Time Bomb Memo Filed on Home State Savings by ODSL Examiner in Early 1983

I have deliberately retained the working copy of this examination report several days past the mandatory five-day deadline because it is my understanding that the new Superintendent will not formally assume his duties in the office until the end of the second week in February.

I respectfully submit that the new Superintendent should be alerted to the veritable time-bomb that is ticking away in this association. Briefly stated, the problems can be summarized in the following two sentences. In June 1982 the association borrowed $84 million for one year from a small investment firm called E.S.M. Government Securities, Inc. located in Fort Lauderdale, Florida. As collateral for this borrowed money, the association assigned to E.S.M.'s control various types of securities which the association had bought for $209 million.

As stated in my examination report of July 10, 1982, should E.S.M. be unable for any reason to redeliver the securities in June 1983, the association will be confronted with a loss of $125 million. If that happens, the association's savings depositors will be required to bear a considerable portion of the loss. The association's net worth is less than $12 million and the total assets of the Ohio Deposit Guarantee Fund, of which the association is a member, are only about $65 million. The association does not have FSLIC insurance.

An association's loss exposure in transactions of this type should never exceed its net worth.

In view of former Superintendent Wideman's perfunctory letter transmitting this report to the association, I would appreciate receiving a copy of the board of directors' response when it is received.

Sylvester F. Hentschel

February 8, 1983

Table 5-2 COMPARISON OF WEIGHTED-AVERAGE EXPLICIT DEPOSIT
INTEREST RATES AT HOME STATE SAVINGS AND FSLIC-
INSURED SAVINGS INSTITUTIONS AT SELECTED DATES,
1978–85 (percent per annum)

Year		Home State	FSLIC-Insured Institutions
A. Calendar-Year Figures, 1978–82			
1978		7.2	6.52
1979		8.7	7.31
1980		10.1	8.69
1981	H1	11.7	10.05
	H2	13.3	11.34
1982		11.4	11.03
B. Monthly Average Figures at ODSL Reporting Dates, 1980–85			
6/30/80		10.5	9.05
6/30/81		12.1	10.74
6/30/82		13.0	11.22
9/30/83		10.4	9.40
4/30/85		9.8	9.22

Sources: ODSL examination reports on Home State Savings given in the
Appendix to the OJSC testimony of Sylvester Hentschel; figures for
FSLIC-insured institutions are from *'82 Savings and Loan Sourcebook* and
'85 and *'86 Savings Institution Sourcebook*.

insurance guarantees. In turn, the value of these guarantees did not
rest on the accumulated reserves of state and federal deposit-insurance agencies. At all deposit-insurance agencies, reserves had fallen
below the value of the unrealized losses that a careful analyst would
assess to be potential claims against these reserves. Rather, the value
of these guarantees depended on the conjecture that, in a crisis,
incumbent politicians (no matter what their party affiliations happened to be) would invariably find it in their joint interest to recapitalize insolvent deposit-insurance funds.

The ODGF's weakness degenerated into a meltdown precisely because, during the run on Home State and in its immediate aftermath,
the applicability of depositors' rational conjecture was undermined
in three ways. First, anyone familiar with the information system
that state regulators had to work with recognized that the governor's
assurances as to the solvency of Home State and the adequacy of
ODGF reserves clearly exceeded his capacity to know. This raised
doubts about his veracity and his financial acumen. Second, his

Table 5-3 CHRONOLOGY OF REGULATORY GAMBLING DURING
ODGF'S LOSS-GENERATION STAGE

July 22, 1980. Examination of Home State uncovers violation in the extent
of nondeposit borrowing underway (including reverse repos).

August 24–28, 1981. At a training seminar, ODSL examiners learn ESM
has poor standing with FHL Bank of Chicago. Follow-up meetings
between ESM managers and ODSL officials fuel doubts about Home
State's repo business with ESM.

June 2, 1982. Home State concentration of repo business with ESM clearly
surfaces as an issue at Ohio regulatory agency. Called a "time bomb" in
draft examination report in October 1982 by Sylvester Hentschel, who
assigns the firm the ODSL's lowest rating. According to the ODSL
Manual of Examinations, "This rating is reserved for institutions with
major and serious problems which management appears to be unable or
unwilling to correct."

October, 1982–February 1985. Examiners' recommendations to stop
branch expansion and take other tough measures are regularly
overridden by successive ODSL superintendents. The superintendent
who retired in early 1985 reported that he sought specific guidance
through channels from higher authorities. Home State managers
repeatedly promise to reduce their exposure to losses in ESM and find
fairly lame ways to renege on these promises. The ODGF regularly
approves the payment of dividends by Home State.

March 4, 1985. ESM fails and proves $300 to $350 million short. Effect on
ODGF parallels the effect that the Bevil, Bresler, and Schulman failure
in May had on Maryland S&Ls.

Source: Kane (1988).

political ties to Home State's chief executive officer raised the possibility that conflicts of interest might be clouding his judgment.
Third and most important, partly because of partisan skirmishing,
the governor and legislature simultaneously refused to backstop ODGF
losses in the Home State failure and contributed only $50 million
of state funds to a successor fund that was being asked to guarantee
almost $4 billion in deposits at the 70 surviving S&Ls. Depositors of
economically insolvent former ODGF member firms saw these actions as an attempt to get the Ohio taxpayer off the hook for unrealized losses at their firms, too. Even though engaging in a run on
these institutions cost a depositor the sure time and trouble of standing in line and establishing new depository connections, it would
cut off his (or her) exposure to losses from this unexpected turn in
state financial policy. Net returns to an individual from engaging in

a run would grow with the size of his deposit balance and with his perception of the size of the unbooked insolvency at his state-insured S&L. For all depositors, the incentive to withdraw deposit balances became stronger as state politicians tried to pass the buck.

The Maryland Case

The proximate cause of the demise of the Maryland Savings-Share Insurance Corporation (MSSIC) was a depositor run on two deeply insolvent clients: the $839 million Old Court S&L and the $370 million Merritt Commercial S&L. The string of losses that ruined these institutions had three sources: (1) defaults on reverse repurchase agreements made by a securities firm that went bankrupt on April 8, 1985; (2) a go-for-broke growth strategy of high-risk loans fueled by high deposit interest rates; and (3) violations of regulatory and corporate controls on loan and investment decisions.

Table 5.4 shows that for years, MSSIC received evidence of repeated rules violations and criminal acts by officers associated with these firms. Several top officers of these institutions have since been convicted or pled guilty to embezzlement or misappropriation of corporate funds. Regulators' failure to penalize these officers in stern and timely fashion for violating ethical and regulatory norms of conduct represents a chain of regulatory gambles. MSSIC officials claim that their failure to impose tough penalties was justified by the need to avoid actions that might generate publicity unfavorable enough to trigger a run on these and other MSSIC institutions. It may also be that their reluctance to discipline wayward clients was reinforced by bad legal advice. It happens that, during the loss-generation period, MSSIC and several of its troublesome clients were being advised by the same law firm. In 1987, this firm paid $27 million to settle a state-initiated malpractice suit for sustaining this conflict of interest.

Rumors of MSSIC weakness grew stronger and stronger after the failure of the ODGF. Nevertheless, MSSIC officials continued to gamble that they could keep sailing a rapidly sinking ship. They refused to take the needed political and economic medicine of shoring up their firm's net worth and strengthening their information, monitoring, and enforcement subsystems. Instead, MSSIC officials promoted the topsy-turvy idea that for the Maryland legislature to prepare publicly for a run would undermine faith in the MSSIC guarantees and generate more trouble than it would save.

Rumors that a deposit institution or its insurer are insolvent are hard to refute when reliable information on their current financial

Table 5-4 CHRONOLOGY OF REGULATORY GAMBLING PRIOR TO THE
MARYLAND SAVINGS-SHARE INSURANCE CORPORATION
CRISIS

1. Loss Generation and Repeated Regulatory Forbearance

November, 1962. Maryland Savings-Share Insurance Corporation (MSSIC) begins operations. Members required to have net worth equal to 4% of "free share accounts."

March 24, 1976. MSSIC board adopts by-law providing that MSSIC's insurance limit for "each separate account" of any association could not exceed the FSLIC limit by more than $10,000. Prior to 1976, coverage was determined by aggregating accounts with same owner *by depositor*, as FSLIC does.

May 25, 1978. MSSIC letter to First Progressive states that, as an officer of First Progressive, Jeffrey Levitt had diverted association funds to his own use.

July, 1981. MSSIC signs as "Insurance Agreement" with Old Court restricting its managers' freedom because the association's net worth had fallen below MSSIC's 3% trigger for such actions.

Sometime in 1982. Using a MSSIC-approved $2.2 million loan from First Progressive, Jeffrey Levitt and Allan Pearlstein solidify their control of First Progressive, which was operating under a MSSIC Insurance Agreement.

Sometime in 1983. Old Court and Progressive embark on aggressive growth strategy, fueling rapid asset growth by offering high interest rates to depositors.

May 6, 1983. Maryland S&L Division examiners report numerous irregularities and violations of Division and MSSIC rules in connection with Old Court's program of high-risk lending.

February, 1984. MSSIC learns that First Progressive had made unauthorized investments with the approval of Levitt.

April, 1984. Examination of Old Court shows continuing violations of MSSIC rules.

April 23, 1984. Managerial obligations under the Insurance Agreement with Old Court are terminated after Old Court prepays its subordinated debenture to MSSIC.

May, 1984. MSSIC board discusses significant financial deterioration of First Progressive of Westminster, Maryland and cites Old Court as "responsible at least in part." Preliminary examination by the S&L Division reveals "very weak operational standards" at both institutions.

August, 1984. MSSIC board notes that Old Court is growing rapidly by writing primarily large construction loans funded by jumbo CDs and exceeding agency's guidelines on the proportion of assets invested in such loans.

continues

Table 5-4 CHRONOLOGY OF REGULATORY GAMBLING PRIOR TO THE
MARYLAND SAVINGS-SHARE INSURANCE CORPORATION
CRISIS Continued

1. Loss Generation and Repeated Regulatory Forbearance Continued

August, 1984. MSSIC staff recommends that Board direct Old Court by
letter to cease and desist from further construction and land loan
commitments.

November 1, 1984. Progressive is merged into Old Court.

December 12, 1984. MSSIC membership committee unanimously
recommends that the Board issue a cease and desist order to Old Court.

2. Escalating Testing of Fund Resources

January 20, 1985. 60 Minutes carries segment on insolvency of Nebraska
guaranty fund. Generates subsequent unease among MSSIC depositors.

February 27, 1985. MSSIC's Board resolves to subject Old Court to a cease
and desist order and to require it to enter into an Operating Agreement.
The cease and desist order is never issued and the Operating
Agreement is not signed until April 23, 1985.

March 8, 1985. Home State Savings Bank is closed, rendering the Ohio
Deposit Guaranty Fund insolvent.

March 16, 1985. MSSIC officials persuade administration officials to force
withdrawal of General Assembly House Bill 1609, requiring all 102
MSSIC institutions to state in their ads that they are not backed by the
full faith and credit of the state.

March 22, 1985. MSSIC sends cease-and-desist letter to Merritt Board
indicating criminal activity. Letter is not shared with federal officials
until May 2.

March 25, 1985. Head of MSSIC circulates a reassuring memo to
membership about MSSIC's reaction to the Ohio crisis.

April 8, 1985. Bevil, Bresler & Schulman Asset Management Corp. closes,
imposing losses on MSSIC's second-largest institution, $839 mil. Old
Court Savings and Loan and on $370 mil. Merritt Commerical Savings
and Loan. These institutions proceed to experience the first consumer
run of MSSIC crisis.

April 11, 1985. Officials from Maryland Attorney General's office prepare
memorandum mentioning difficulty in getting accurate information
from state S&L division and MSSIC and recommending Governor to
have "face-to-face" meetings to obtain facts. A third MSSIC S&L
(Chesapeake) joins Chevy Chase S&L and Baltimore Country S&L in
openly applying for FSLIC insurance.

April 16, 1985. Federal officials alert Governor's staff to a "silent run" on
MSSIC institutions of $375 million over the previous two months.
Roughly $7 billion still in MSSIC institutions.

Table 5-4 *Continued*

2. Escalating Testing of Fund Resources *Continued*

April 29, 1985. First of the "major crisis meetings" of Federal Reserve and
FHLBB officials with Governor Hughes, his staff, state regulators, and
top state lawyers. Feds predict a major run and describe some
associations as at the "end of their ropes," giving special attention to
the sorry state of Old Court. Officials from MSSIC and state S&L
Division claim that installing new CEO at Old Court "would take care
of it."

May 2, 1985. Second "crisis meeting." Federal officials are stunned to
learn of previously withheld March 22 MSSIC letter. Conservatorship
lawsuits considered for Old Court and Merritt.

May 2–8, 1985. Old Court continues to solicit deposits via radio
advertisements, stressing the "Old Court advantage" of high interest
rates, despite Attorney General's behind-the-scenes efforts to stop these
ads as violations of the state's Consumer Protection Act.

May 8, 1985. Third "crisis meeting," this time without Governor Hughes,
who was in Israel. Old Court management change decided upon and
press release drafted.

May 9, 1985. The *Baltimore Sun* runs story unfavorable to Old Court.
Runs on Old Court offices accelerate. Criminal investigation into Merritt
is formally announced.

May 10, 1985. Merritt loses $3 million in deposits in a Saturday morning
run.

May 13, 1985. Old Court put into state-controlled conservatorship. New
run begins at Merritt.

May 14, 1985. Governor Hughes proclaims a state of public crisis and
emergency and imposes a $1,000-per-month limit on depositor
withdrawals at MSSIC institutions. Discloses to reporters that 20 MSSIC
institutions experienced a $630 million withdrawal over last few
months.

Source: Kane (1988) (adapted primarily from Preston 1986).

conditions simply does not exist. In the short term, authorities can
most reliably maintain confidence *not* by mindlessly denying and
covering up the insolvency, but by demonstrating their willingness
to back up the troubled entity. The more likely it becomes that politicians will fail to cover the losses of any class of depositor in full
and in short order, the greater the possibility of serious runs by
depositors in that class. Prudence tells depositors who feel themselves at risk to move their funds when credible flows of adverse

information occur and/or other depositors are running. If the troubled institution either turns out to be solvent or is bailed out with public funds, ex-depositors lose only the time and trouble of switching their business to a new firm. But if it is eventually closed on disadvantageous terms, the percentage exposure to loss of every depositor who does not switch increases with every dollar of other deposits that escapes from the firm before its demise becomes official.

REGULATORY COVERUP AND GAMBLING IN RADIOACTIVE WASTE

Taxpayers' exposure to losses from an incentive-incompatible deposit-insurance fund may be likened metaphorically to their exposure to fallout from improperly shielded nuclear waste. Ironically, evidence has surfaced that at several hundred nuclear processing and weapons sites, government officials have knowingly permitted massive quantities of radioactive waste to leak into the neighboring soil, groundwater, and atmosphere (e.g., Alvarez and Makhijani 1988).

Lax standards for handling nuclear materials and for protecting the health of neighbors and employees at these sites correspond to lax enforcement of taxpayers' interest in deposit-insurance funds. The costs of adequately cleaning up these sites parallels the cost of recapitalizing FSLIC. Given these parallels, evidence of conscious regulatory gambling by government officials responsible for overseeing nuclear processing and weapons plants may be interpreted as providing further support for the incentive-breakdown hypothesis.

The case I know best is the Fernald nuclear-weapons plant (located 18 miles from Cincinnati, Ohio). Court documents establish that officials overseeing the plant knew *for decades* that they were discharging thousands of tons of radioactive waste into the neighboring environment. These discharges took the forms of smokestack emissions, liquid runoffs, and evaporation. The biggest problem was that waste was stored in ground storage pits located in wet areas that government geologists had declared to be unsuitable. Water covering the pits would become contaminated and would be pumped into the Great Miami River.

When neighbors learned of their exposure, they began to accumulate evidence of: (1) above-average cancer rates for persons in the vicinity of the plant, and (2) systematic falsification of the past vironmental-impact tests that were conducted at the plant. Moreover, researchers from Miami University found a variety of genetic deformities and abnormal growth patterns in plants and animals living near the Fernald installation. Confronted with this evidence, government spokespersons justified the coverup as forced upon them by Congress' unwillingness to appropriate clean-up funds. They challenged the presumption that their decisions had caused cancer or other abnormalities by noting that the fact of repeated radioactive discharges does not strictly prove that people or other life forms were specifically harmed by the discharges.

SUMMARY AND TRANSITION

Concealing deposit-insurance subsidies from taxpayers makes the long-run effects of these subsidies destabilizing, in that this deprives taxpayers of knowledge they need to play the disciplinary role that stockholders and creditors fulfill in a private firm. In July 1988, Congress was considering a bill to require private firms that sell services with the help of names or symbols similar to those used by federal agencies to disclose clearly their nonofficial status. The point is that incorporating the word "federal" into the title of a private corporation is misleading on its face. The difference between such private firms and FSLIC was nicely (if inadvertently) summarized by a government spokesperson (*Wall Street Journal*, July 6, 1988, p. 23): "When you're misleading [sic] the public, there's a line. Most of these groups go way over the line."

A need to obtain public esteem and approval helps to explain officials' decisions to seek political or appointive office. The ODGF, MSSIC, and FSLIC cases provide evidence that a sense of shame underlies the deposit-insurance subsidy-production process. In each case, givers and receivers of subsidies have devoted considerable energy to packaging their dealings in forms that prove hard for the public to see and hard to measure even when seen. Preserving at least the appearance of a public servant's personal honor and integrity is an important goal, one that ranks above merely winning re-election or holding on to a particular job. Whether or not an official explicitly worries about potential career fallout from tough decisions, the chance to engage in a postgovernment settling up for periods of underpaid government service forms an important part of the implicit compensation earned by top government officials. A better informed electorate might or might not force career penalties on regulatory and legislative rascals. Nevertheless, requiring authorities to provide appropriate evidence of how well public responsibilities are being handled would have the salutary effect of lessening the salary that a poor regulator could command in postgovernment employment.

That politically powerful groups can extract government subsidies is inherent in the American system of mixed enterprise. No one should suppose that improving the flow of information about financial regulatory performance can end subsidy extraction altogether. A more limited goal is promoted in the guidelines for reform developed in the next chapter: merely to make the production of deposit-insurance subsidies more painful to those who benefit from their creation.

Designing financial regulatory structures that work *with* rather than *against* efficient client adaptation provides the best chance of achieving society's long-run regulatory goals. First and foremost, this means preventing regulators and regulatees from distorting with impunity the flow of information by which taxpayers assess their performance and finances.

The initial unwillingness of state authorities to back the ODGF and MSSIC reflects their closeness to taxpayers. State politicians recognized that state taxpayers had not seen themselves as risk-bearers of last resort. However, at the federal level, taxpayer obligations are more diffuse. Not until after the election of 1988 did FSLIC guarantees become a pressing political issue. Even today, the high cost of providing FDIC guarantees to troubled commercial banks is receiving almost no popular attention at all.

Note

1. This section draws heavily on Kane (1988)

References

Alvarez, Robert, and Arjun Makhijani. 1988. "Radioactive Waste: Hidden Legacy of the Arms Race." *Technology Review* (August/September), pp. 41–51.

Barth, James R., R. Dan Brumbaugh, Jr., Daniel Sauerhaft, and George H.K. Wang. 1986. "Failure Costs of Government-Regulated Financial Firms: The Case of Thrift Institutions." Washington: Federal Home Loan Bank Board.

Kane, Edward J. 1987. "Dangers of Capital Forbearance: The Case of The FSLIC and 'Zombie' S&Ls." *Contemporary Policy Issues* 5 (January), pp. 77–83.

_____. 1988. "How Incentive-Incompatible Deposit-Insurance Funds Fail." Prochnow Report No. PR-014. Madison, Wis.: The Prochnow Educational Foundation.

Preston, Wilbur D., Jr. 1986. *Report on the Maryland Savings and Loan Crisis to the Maryland General Assembly by Special Counsel.* Annapolis (Jan. 8).

Chapter Six

GUIDELINES FOR SALIENT REFORM

In public policy, as in medicine and automobile repair, diagnosis must precede prescription. Only by understanding what went wrong can policymakers reasonably hope to put things right again.

The link between diagnosis and prescription makes it vital to understand not only how large the bill for FSLIC has become, but how and when it came to be so large. The diagnosis I spell out in previous chapters implies that it is not enough for taxpayers to ask Congress to set up a sensible financing plan for paying off FSLIC's accumulated bill. They must also ask for a system of controls on future backdoor spending by the deposit-insurance bureaucracy strong enough to prevent a replay. Taxpayers should not be asked to confront such a bill again.

Qualified experts may disagree about how to fix the federal deposit insurance system, even with the same diagnosis of what is wrong. But differences in the individual remedies recommended by experts with similar diagnoses resemble differences in medical treatment strategies recommended by different doctors. Ordinarily, many different combinations of specific treatment options can remedy or ease a given set of difficulties. While strategic differences in therapeutic approaches are often important, differences in tactical details may have only minor effects. The great danger is that, in sorting through alternative diagnoses of the deposit-insurance problem, authorities will look for easy ways out. They may be attracted to inadequate diagnoses because they are easy to grasp and imply politically painless solutions, with too little concern for how incompletely they explain the mess that has developed.

This book has repeatedly attacked two dangerously simplified diagnoses. The first may be called the "bad-apples hypothesis." This hypothesis holds that the thrift mess reflects the nation's bad luck in having suddenly developed a concentration of bad and dishonest managers in a single industry. Subscribers to this analysis see the issue as one of identifying the "bad apples," and keeping them and others like them out of the industry in the future. On this opinion, the major reforms needed are tougher criminal and civil penalties for fraud and mismanagement by managers of financial institutions.

The bad-apples model attributes thrift institution losses predominantly to bad management and fraud induced in effect by inadequate legal penalties. But this theory fails to explain why managerial mistakes and frauds burgeoned at thrift institutions in the 1980s. The deeper question that a complete theory must answer is why were the penalties too low in the 1980s, but not before? The deposit-insurance incentive-breakdown hypothesis transforms this question and answers it. The transformation involves noting: (1) that much of what can loosely be called fraudulent reporting of a troubled firm's earnings and financial condition is completely legal under GAAP and RAP accounting, and (2) that the bulk of what can be loosely called managerial mistakes were also clever gambles that were fostered by incentive defects in the provision of federal deposit insurance. The answer to the question of why longstanding legal penalties against what the bad-apples theory deems to be fraud and mismanagement became ineffective in the 1980s is that, as a firm becomes decapitalized, the rewards from engaging in loose and strict forms of these behaviors become progressively larger.

The second misdiagnosis may be called the "excessive deregulation hypothesis." This is the view that FSLIC and its client institutions were ruined by decisions Congress made in 1980 and 1982 to relax various longstanding constraints on how thrifts could operate. Adherents to this view imply that thrift-institution managers lack the business acumen both to make appropriate decisions about the explicit interest rates they can afford to pay on deposits and to exercise prudently the wider range of asset powers established by the financial reform acts of 1980 and 1982.

This false diagnosis ignores the fact that widespread insolvencies predated the alleged decisive mistake of letting thrifts compete closely with banks. The implied therapy is threefold: paying FSLIC's bill, restricting thrift charters as before, and reinstituting ceilings on thrift deposit rates. The most glaring problem with this therapy is that it would constrain only a few of the many ways that an aggressive deposit-institution manager can extract future subsidies to risk taking from deposit insurance. It would not alter incentives for officials to cover up and defer action on insolvencies that develop on their watch, or for insolvent institutions to fashion go-for-broke plays.

This reform strategy would not even limit the major ways that narrowly chartered thrift institutions undertook ruinous plays in the 1970s. Such plays typically involved financing the firm's mortgage portfolio in a massively short-funded way. An important further issue concerns the harmful side effects that this "cure" threatens to have on the future viability of the portion of the thrift industry that is healthy today. As shown in chapter one, thrifts have faced a declining earnings spread in mortgage lending during recent years. The downward trend in this spread traces not just to the aggressiveness of zombie institutions, but also to the way that the growing competition from mortgage-backed securities has passed free federal credit support routinely accorded government-sponsored mortgage-financing corporations through into lower yields on home mortgages (Kane and Foster 1986). The narrowness of the existing spread makes it likely that a goodly number of currently healthy thrifts could not earn a decent living if they were forced entirely back into traditional patterns of industry operation.

THE IMMEDIATE PROBLEM

In a currently popular song, a singer implores her listeners to "shove me in the shallow waters before I get too deep." Taxpayers' immediate problem is less a matter of paying FSLIC's bills than of getting zombie and potential zombie firms repaired or off the street, and doing this at minimum total cost to federal taxpayers.

Appropriate insolvency resolution requires that the lender of last resort avoid lending to insolvent institutions and that the insurer's decision to pull the plug on individual firms be given greater insulation from political pressure. The Bush Initiative recognizes that to strengthen the FDIC-FSLIC management team politically, it must first be strengthened financially. It must be assigned sufficient resources to support the charge-offs inherent in taking over client institutions before their capital is exhausted. It must also receive enough budgetary freedom to hire the staff it needs to carry out the tasks of enforcing solvency requirements and of bridging the operation of decapitalized firms until private acquirers or investors can be found. To make sure that solvency decisions are objective and economically based, authorities and industry leaders must accept a more meaningful concept of legal insolvency. The criterion developed must focus on the market value of each client's enterprise-contributed capital. Insolvency cannot be permitted to turn on an institution's liquidity because liquidity either is enhanced by federal deposit guarantees or, in truly severe cases, becomes a function of discretionary eligibility criteria laid down by the lender of last resort. Nor can the insolvency test be permitted to focus on traditional GAAP accounting measures of a firm's net worth. This value too is inflated by federal guarantees, and existing accounting rules leave firms and regulators considerable opportunity to self-interestedly conceal evidence of insolvency.

Prior to the announcement of the Bush plan in early February 1989, the political debate over FSLIC focused itself less on how to recapitalize zombie thrifts efficiently than on a series of politically cosmetic, but economically irrelevant points. It is useful to explain the irrelevance of these cosmetic issues to clear the way for a discussion of effective measures.

Four Distracting Cosmetic Issues

The first cosmetic issue concerns an alleged need to keep FSLIC's losses from increasing the national debt. Because FSLIC is obligated to repay every dollar of insured deposits at insolvent thrifts, the bill for its losses is effectively (i.e., implicitly) already part of the national debt. Properly construed, the debt and the deficit include *de facto* as well as *de jure* obligations of Treasury resources. Entering FSLIC's obligations explicitly on the books of the Treasury would increase neither the true federal deficit nor the true national debt. All that is at issue is converting into an explicit (or formal) obligation what is already an implicit (or *de facto*) Treasury obligation, one that has been affirmed in two joint congressional resolutions and in reassuring public statements by President Bush.

The second cosmetic issue focuses on a supposed long fight to keep taxpayers from bearing any of the burden of bailing out FSLIC. Pride in having kept "federal money" out of the FSLIC bailout process as long as possible reflects and perpetuates longstanding forms of accounting deception and defective economic analysis. Implicit federal expenditures have been made on behalf of FSLIC for years and in substantial amounts. These expenditures have two main components. The first and largest part consists of annual financing costs implied by the Treasury's conjectural obligation to support FSLIC debt to keep FSLIC from permanently defaulting on any of its diverse corporate obligations. The second part consists of tax benefits that have for years been accorded routinely to acquirers of failing thrifts.

These benefits have two elements: (1) a right to carry forward the acquired thrifts' past losses and to deduct them against the acquirer's other taxable income, and (2) full or partial exemption from federal income taxation of FSLIC assistance payments. These tax forgivenesses represent collectible tax revenues that could have been sent to the Treasury and shipped to FSLIC for explicit disbursement. Explicit Treasury revenues are reduced by the amount of any tax forgiveness and an equal implicit expenditure is incurred. Envisioning the Treasury as effectively handing uncollected tax funds directly back to the institutions to which FSLIC directed the tax forgivenesses serves to clarify that the values that are transferred are federal tax monies.

The third cosmetic question turned on the alleged sacredness of past congressional pledges to control federal spending. Using concerns about keeping explicit federal outlays low under Gramm-Rudman-Hollings legislative provisions to control the deficit as an excuse for engaging in unnecessarily costly off-budget financing schemes and for keeping a large number of zombie thrifts in play promotes false economy. Decisions which are penny-wise and pound-foolish pervert the very idea of budget discipline. It would be tragic for Congress to employ the letter of the Gramm-Rudman-Hollings law to violate its very spirit. To be meaningful, budget discipline must apply to implicit and explicit expenditures alike. The more that the interest rates paid by off-balance-sheet funding corporations exceed Treasury interest rates, the longer that authorities permit zombie and near-zombie firms to survive without recapitalization, and the larger the number of firms allowed to operate in this way, the higher becomes the taxpayers' bill for cleaning up FSLIC's past mistakes.

The fourth distracting issue concerns the relative importance of George Bush's campaign pledge to impose "no new taxes." This promise threatens to become yet another excuse for deferring an adequate refinancing of FSLIC obligations. Initial skirmishing over the Bush administration's January 1989 proposal to retire FSLIC's shortage over time from the proceeds of a 25 or 30 basis-point charge on customer deposits at banks, S&Ls, and credit unions was instructive. The debate focused on the semantic issue of whether the charge should or should not be construed as a "tax." Administration efforts to portray the charge as a long overdue modernization of "user fees" for federal deposit insurance, and to refute their opponents' claim that it could reasonably be interpreted as an excise tax, struck a note of intellectual slipperiness that helped to harden opposition to this measure.

The irony of these cosmetic issues is that focusing on them allowed the same failures in government accounting that helped the FSLIC bill to grow so large in the first place to interfere with settling FSLIC accounts in an economically efficient manner. The fundamental issues in paying the FSLIC bill are only two: (1) how to assure that taxpayers get full value for every dollar they put up, and (2) how to distribute the burden of providing these dollars both over time and across various types of federal taxpayers. Gramm-Rudman-Hollings provisions and the no-tax pledge should not be allowed to become counterproductive (i.e., cost-increasing) constraints on how efficiently these issues are resolved. Not appropriating or borrowing resources adequate for the job resembles asking emergency-room personnel to use only 40 feet of sutures to close every hundred feet of open wounds brought to them for treatment. It makes more sense to send out for additional surgical thread than to sew up only two inches of every five-inch wound.

Who Should Pay?

Who will finally put up the funds used to pay FSLIC's bill is a question that generates considerable conflict. The fundamental questions in such conflict concern two dimensions of fairness: (1) relative responsibility for generating the bill, and (2) relative ability to pay.

Trying to apportion the bill according to who is to blame for it is an impossible task. As I have emphasized repeatedly, there is more than enough blame to go around. No one is truly innocent. Even apparently innocent households can be faulted for not leaning on Congress long ago to enforce their interest in minimizing taxpayer exposure to future losses in FSLIC.

Deciding how to finance government expenditures is inherently a political task. It is natural not to want to pay higher taxes and, other things equal, to want to put off paying bills when one can. These political realities make it clear that appropriating the resources to eliminate zombie thrifts requires Congress and the president to work out a package of debt and tax financing that is simultaneously politically acceptable and large enough to do the job.

Economic analysis can help by clarifying that some taxes and forms of debt tend to be more efficient and distributed more "fairly" than others. For example, economic analysis can show that trying to pay FSLIC's accumulated bill entirely from the proceeds of a user fee or excise tax on deposits at selected classes of financial institutions would probably not work. Given that the fee would have to exceed the level required to fund continuing guarantees, the effective base for this fee or tax would decrease over time. Some of these institutions' former business would be diverted to other classes of firms, and the class of firms being taxed would be led to substitute non-deposit forms of debt for deposits. Similarly, because the level of the charge would exceed the value of the guarantees conveyed to individual institutions, economics would not support the political effort to label it a user fee.

But economics cannot make a choice that is essentially a matter for political negotiation. What is needed is a will to negotiate. After years of deferring FSLIC's losses to the indefinite future, a decision to act now can only develop from an understanding of how very costly it is to taxpayers as a group to allow zombie firms to continue in operation with federal guarantees.

Waiting for the *de jure* insolvency of a federal insurer to trigger a congressional debate about loss distribution is an irresponsible political strategy. Such a debate figures to prolong the associated industry crisis and to cause unnecessary anxiety to households whose assets might be frozen. The anxiety would be particularly acute for older households who often rely on deposits to finance their routine expenditures. This possibility makes the existence of an incipient deposit-insurer insolvency a matter of grave concern and creates a need to narrow the odds that one of the federal deposit insurers might actually experience a *de jure* insolvency. Making the nation's backup taxpayer-guarantors clearly aware of the size and nature of their potential liabilities in FSLIC may be the only way to build a coalition for deposit insurance reform.

The central point in the case for long-run reform is the likelihood that informed taxpayers would not willingly have accepted the burden that misreported deposit-insurer promises have inefficiently foisted upon them. Each successive increment in the extent of an insurer's guarantees becomes increasingly expensive to attain. In their individual insurance transactions, taxpayers habitually select automobile policies that include deductibles and major medical and surgical coverages that include participating coinsurance elements and limitations on cumulative payouts. This shows individuals' informed response to the high incremental costs of supporting complete coverages. It strains credulity to believe that citizens who are willing to accept substantial amounts of risk everywhere else in their portfolios would knowingly choose to pay the freight for virtually complete guarantees of the small subset of funds they and their fellow citizens choose to hold in bank and thrift deposits.

The inefficiency of complete guarantees implies that the completeness should be phased out. But it is important to phase out existing guarantees intelligently. Simply to abandon them in the midst of a potential crisis would undermine public confidence.

De Facto Nationalization[1]

When one recognizes the value to FSLIC of the federal guarantees that the public presumes or conjectures that FSLIC enjoys, neither zombie thrifts nor FSLIC itself is truly economically insolvent. But a threat of insolvency exists, in that the current informal nature of the Treasury's guarantees makes them less than perfectly reliable and encourages the public to test their quality. In other words, as a matter of law though not necessarily as a matter of fact, if FSLIC were to default, depositors at insolvent institutions would have to pick up the shortfall in FSLIC reserves. This encourages "deposit runs" because an uninsured depositor's individual exposure to loss depends on the depositor's place in the deposit-redemption queue.

To the extent that the FSLIC's capacity to make good on its guarantees begins to be widely doubted, two things occur:

1. FSLIC-insured thrifts have to pay higher deposit rates or lose funds as an industry to other institutions—especially to commercial banks and conservatively run money-market mutual funds; and
2. The market value of the unbooked FSLIC guarantees falls, undermining the *de facto* economic solvency of the industry.

Firming up and redefining U.S. Treasury guarantees of FSLIC obligations (i.e., recapitalizing the FSLIC and the thrift industry) must play a central part in any effective program of deposit-insurance reform. This requires a full-faith-and-credit statute. The political difficulty of accepting the responsibility for FSLIC's accumulated losses in such a way is underscored by the unwillingness of previous Congresses and administrations to appropriate explicit resources for this task.

Although on any given day the probability remains extremely small that depositor runs will melt down FSLIC, if the current system is maintained over the indefinite future, the occurrence of a breakdown in FSLIC finances seems nearly inevitable. Moreover, even if a breakdown can be avoided, the government has accumulated a large and growing equity stake in deposit institutions that amounts to a *de facto* nationalization.

De facto nationalization occurs when the affairs of the insolvent firm pass directly or indirectly under the control of a federal bureau. As with firms operating under a strict supervisory agreement, insurers sometimes soften the fact of nationalization by: (1) disguising their ownership position as uncompensated forbearance or as an options or warrant position, and (2) by contracting with a third party to manage the firm. De facto nationalization has so far been conceived as a temporary step, meant to permit the deposit insurer to search for acceptable private bids for the institution's charter over a less pressing time frame. For example, this is the justification authorities offered in 1984 for the de facto nationalization of Continental Illinois. In this disguised nationalization, the FDIC took a large options position in the firm's stock. Five years later, the FDIC still retains approximately a 41 percent interest in this firm.

Reversing effective ownership positions has absorbed substantial time and effort. During the 1980s, FSLIC has engaged in temporary de facto nationalization in two different ways. In 1982, the agency evolved a form of joint conservatorship known as the phoenix plan. This plan was employed in seven cases in which it proved possible to combine several insolvent firms in a given region into a single corporation. Each phoenix corporation was recapitalized by FSLIC, which in turn appointed some or all of the firm's board of directors. In 1986, FSLIC may arguably be said to have reprivatized the last two of these institutions. But in the meantime, their place in de facto nationalization has been taken by more than 100 institutions enlisted into a successor scheme known as the management consignment program. In this program, FSLIC appoints new directors and assigns the management of the corporation to a team of executives assembled by a healthy savings institution or other private contractor (which the insurer may have had to cajole or pressure into taking on the job). Although it usually does not formally recapitalize the successor corporation, FSLIC's deeper involvement in the firm conjecturally strengthens its informal guarantees. Both programs have the advantage of taking the original stockholders and managers of the failed institution out of the game, thereby permitting FSLIC to balance its preexisting asymmetric position by taking over the upside of bets it is already guaranteeing. Such temporary trusteeships also permit a more graceful evaluation and unwinding of the troubled firm's detailed losses.

Because the universe of potential private buyers for individual institutions has proved restricted in practice, buying time to develop a reliable balance sheet makes a great deal of sense, particularly in reprivatizing large institutions. What doesn't make sense is not requiring insured institutions to develop and maintain such balance sheets as a matter of course. Moreover, two other points need to be recognized: (1) during periods of temporary nationalization formal linkage to the deposit insurer may give nationalized deposit institutions competitive advantages in particular markets, and (2) interim managements face various conflicts of interest and strong incentives to pay an excessive price for deposit funds. Given FSLIC officials' own principal-agent conflicts (exemplified by insurers' efforts to distort the flow of information to taxpayers about the adequacy of FSLIC reserves and risk-management activity), it is virtually impossible for them to write a management contract that can give an interim trustee a set of incentives that is fully compatible with the interests of the insurer (see Bisenius, Brumbaugh, and Rogers 1986; Gallagher 1988; Baebel and Golding 1988).

Finally, experience with entities as diverse as Conrail and Continental Illinois suggests that authorities seldom unwind the temporary nationalization of a large institution promptly. This is because squaring up such a firm's affairs almost never occupies an urgent place on the public agenda once it has been nationalized, and is bound in any case to force the insurer to recognize explicitly some embarrassing losses. This argues for setting up a strict timetable for either liquidating nationalized positions or converting them into warrants that have no voting power and a bounded potential for loss.

In the face of our nation's ideological commitment to free markets, it is both tragic and ironic to note that it has unintentionally nationalized a large segment of its deposit-institution industry. By failing to control the value of deposit-insurance guarantees, FSLIC officials have made exercising their option to take over a large bundle of insolvent deposit institutions the only expedient way to balance taxpayers' equity interest in these institutions. The larger this nationalized industry segment is allowed to become before the reprivatization process begins, the greater the potential waste of government operation and the larger the potential for corruption in its reprivatization.

Controlling Potential Inefficiencies in the Reprivatization Process

A good part of the FSLIC bill is now in the form of a de facto equity stake in troubled clients. By not enforcing adequate capital requirements, FSLIC has inadvertently become the nation's largest equity investor in thrift institutions. The need to reprivatize FSLIC's poorly structured and poorly documented equity positions in troubled clients is part and parcel of the FSLIC mess. But disposing of FSLIC's many claims to industry assets raises administrative problems of the first magnitude.

For policy purposes, the value of insurer guarantees needs to be recognized explicitly as an equity position and to be made the centerpiece of an energetic program of reprivatization. At a troubled or aggressively managed thrift, the market value of its FSLIC guarantee looms much larger than enterprise-contributed equity. From the taxpayers' perspective, the value of a FSLIC guarantee is the capitalized value of the net costs that supporting the guarantee imposes on the insurer. To understand these costs and to control their growth, Congress must direct deposit-insurance bureaucrats to prepare an invoice that itemizes them institution by institution. So that taxpayers can readily observe how well the FDIC and FSLIC control their risk exposure, the aggregate value of deposit-insurance guarantees should then be toted up and reported regularly by each guarantor bureau. In unwinding the affairs of zombie and near-zombie firms, the changes in the value of a firm's guarantee should be made the focus of regulatory decisions about forbearance, closure, or recapitalization. The capitalized value of the net costs of supporting deposit-insurance guarantees represents federal taxpayers' equity stake in each troubled thrift. The collection of these stakes deserves to be micromanaged as if it were a portfolio of financial claims formally convertible into common stock. Decisions about which firms regulators should close or restructure, and in what order to treat individual firms, must be designed to bring the growth of the government's unwanted equity stakes in distressed thrifts under control and to see that these stakes are reprivatized without waste or corruption.

The speed and efficiency of reprivatization deserves to be judged by how long it takes, and how much it costs what we may call the "reprivatization bureau" to reduce the guarantee values back to zero. Congress must see how dangerous it would be to force this reprivatization to unfold against the background of deceptive accounting and political, bureaucratic, and deposit-insurance subsidies to risk taking that led to the *de facto* nationalization of so many thrift institutions in the first place. In this distorted environment, FDIC's and FSLIC's past performances as liquidators and as the beneficial owners of institutions placed under their aegis can only be described as discouraging. It is hard to give government liquidators either the incentives or the administrative freedom to squeeze every dollar of liquidation value out of negotiations with potential buyers. Too many restraints are imposed on governmental contracting, budgeting, maximum salaries, and use of incentive compensation. Delays in liquidating insurers' equity holdings, complaints about undue and counterproductive interference, the threat to competing enterprises raised by the possibility that insurer-owned institutions might receive unfair supervisory and regulatory breaks are just some of the temptations and difficulties that regulatory discretion imparts to temporary government ownership. Letting government bureaus control deposit institutions raises issues of accountability, corruption, and inefficiency that our systems of politics and government are not prepared to handle.

The February 1989 Bush Initiative for Corralling Current Zombies

The Bush Initiative of February 6, 1989 focuses on paying the largest part of FSLIC's unpaid bill, by taking over the worst several hundred of the nation's roughly 750 zombies. But the plan is silent on the need to establish accountability for the insolvency-resolution process. Objective procedures must be developed and promulgated to establish: how firms are to be targeted for takeover, liquidation, or merger; how such actions are to be timed; and how to be sure that healthy deposit institutions and other taxpayers get full value for the funds they supply. In the absence of an adequate accountability mechanism, prospects for arbitrariness, waste, and corruption are terrifying.

Accountability exists when decisionmakers are made fully answerable for their decisions. In deposit insurance, this means imposing an itemized and timely informational framework within which officials must report, explain, and justify their decisions to act or not act on individual cases.

Establishing accountability is important because insurers' and Congress' lack of accountability explains decisions made in the past to reduce effective capital requirements for FSLIC thrifts and to *forbear* from taking over individual zombie thrifts when they became decapitalized. This lack of accountability is the crucial defect in public policy that allowed the FSLIC bill to become so large.

Legal insolvency must be redefined so that it turns on the market value of each client's capital without counting the market value of the deposit-insurance guarantees it enjoys. Authorities must employ a concept that measures the true extent of enterprise-contributed capital. At the same time, the deposit-insurance bureaucracy must be required to assess and report regularly its separate risk exposures in healthy, strained, distressed, and insolvent firms. FSLIC officials should have tracked, reported, and minimized their developing risk exposure in the 1970s and 1980s. In fact, as early as 1981 a FSLIC staff member did arrange for me to meet with the head of FSLIC to explain how this could be done. Tables 3-1 and 3-6 in chapter three exemplify the kinds of timely projections of FSLIC's loss exposure its staff could easily have made. Had Congress imposed an accountability for such projections as part of the Garn-St Germain Act in 1982, it and FSLIC officials would have been forced to confront FSLIC's deteriorating situation in 1983, and to recognize it for what it was—a consequence of the economically inappropriate capital-forbearance policies being adopted at this time.

Neglected Portions of FSLIC's Unpaid Bills

The February 1989 Bush Initiative has three principal elements:

1. A proposed estimate of the cost of resolving existing insolvencies at FSLIC-insured thrifts;
2. A financial mechanism for funding this cost from increased explicit deposit-insurance premiums for thrifts and banks and from general tax revenues;
3. A bureaucratic restructuring of the responsibility for resolving thrift insolvencies and for operating the controls used to discipline future risk taking by thrift institutions.

By explicitly funding most of the Treasury's implicit obligation for current zombies, the Bush Initiative greatly improves on previous policies. The Initiative has three major weaknesses, however.

First, resorting to an off-budget financing entity (dubbed the Resolution Funding Corporation) unnecessarily raises the interest cost to be incurred in financing the cleanup. Second, in estimating the problem at $90 billion, the administration has chosen not to reserve—as a private guarantor would—for FSLIC's anticipated loss exposure in hundreds of distressed and strained thrifts whose economic capital is either slightly underwater or only mildly positive. In recent months an upward trend in market interest rates has aggravated the weakness of such firms. Leaving this roughly $45 billion liability unfunded puts an unreasonably large bet on the efficiency of the FDIC's bureaucratic takeover of FSLIC's insolvency-resolution and loss-prevention responsibilities. Finally, the bureaucratic-restructuring part of the plan merely transfers administrative responsibility for taking over, liquidating, or merging zombie thrifts to the FDIC. It presumes disingenuously that the FDIC can readily do two things: (1) accomplish the amazing task of raising weak thrifts' capital to 6 percent of assets by June 1991 and (2) rely on asset-growth limitations, tougher cease and desist powers, and stiffer criminal and civil penalties to restrain future abuse of deposit-insurance guarantees.

The plan's faith in the FDIC to carry these new burdens is its most dangerous feature. It fails to confront either the FDIC's resulting shortages of staff or the deep incentive conflicts that tempted FHLBB officials (with the explicit and implicit encouragement of Congress) to lower effective capital requirements in often tricky ways during the late-1970s and early 1980s. Insolvency resolution would continue to focus on the accounting value of enterprise-contributed capital rather than on its *market value*. Moreover, the proposed legislation fails to impose a *formal obligation* on the FDIC to intervene strongly and predictably into the affairs of capital-deficient firms before exhaustion of the market value of its capital becomes a serious threat.

Handing the ball to the FDIC in this discretionary way maximizes politicians' ability both to continue to pressure regulators to help troubled firms in their constituencies, and to be prepared to blame FDIC officials later for the long-run consequences of this behavior. In years to come, politicians who are scapegoating FSLIC today may scapegoat the FDIC as energetically for regulatory "blunders" whose roots lie in congressionally imposed restraints on what the deposit-insurance bureaucracy can do.

The Initiative's economic weaknesses are best understood as political stratagems. Promulgating a low estimate of the size of FSLIC's problem serves to minimize the impact of insolvency-resolution expenditures on the explicit federal budgets of the next few fiscal years. It also serves to keep the burdens that must be projected for healthy thrifts, commercial banks, and the general taxpayer low enough to make it hard for these parties to feel harmed enough to scuttle the plan. At the same time, continuing to frame as matters for regulatory discretion the issues of what powers an insured firm may exercise, what is capital, and when an institution must be recapitalized or closed maintains congressional opportunities to collect tribute by offering to perform behind-the-scenes "constituent services" for owners and managers of institutions that become decapitalized.

THE LONG-RUN PROBLEM

The long-run problem is to prevent a new generation of deposit-institution zombies from emerging in the future. This means eliminating deposit-insurance subsidies to risk taking. Because these subsidies have woven themselves into the very fabric of federal deposit-institution regulation, no painless way exists to do this. The best that can be done is to target a set of financial, bureaucratic, and political reforms that can efficiently accomplish this task and to design a timetable for phasing in these reforms that moderates the transition costs of adopting the new system.

Those who benefit directly or indirectly from the existing subsidies will fight politically to retain them. Because the subsidies are implicit and hidden, the easiest way to fight their elimination is to fashion and promote superficially appealing misdiagnoses of their causes and effects. For this reason, taxpayers would be wise to insist that the effects of whatever solutions are adopted be capable of being subjected to a battery of continuing market tests.

This book traces the roots of the current deposit-insurance mess to longstanding defects in political and bureaucratic accountability. The overriding problem is that regulatory coverup and forbearance is, at least for strictly self-interested politicians and bureaucrats, the "optimal" response to the emergence of widespread industry insolvency. The current system confronts even the most altruistic authorities with a painful tradeoff between protecting general taxpayers' economic interests and incurring the displeasure of politically strong regulatory clients and their various political allies.

To make this tradeoff less constricting, political-bureaucratic incentives must be structured. To forestall coverups, this restructuring must require that the long-run costs of regulatory forbearances be estimated honestly and released in timely fashion. To lessen opportunities for granting myopic forbearances, market forces or deposit insurers must be required to enforce timely recapitalization of troubled firms.

Improving the Incentive System for Deposit Insurers

The most straightforward way to lessen incentive conflicts for deposit insurers is to impose additional obligations on their managers. As a minimum, these managers need to be made, under penalty of civil or criminal sanction, to do three things.

Accounting Reform. First, they must be required to report regularly on a market-value basis the economic losses imbedded in their operations and commitments and to reserve for these losses appropriately. The governing idea here is to make sure that these enterprises' budgets include implicit (or *de facto*) expenditures as well as explicit items.

Capital Enforcement. Second, they must be required to enforce capital requirements at individual institutions on a market-value basis. Presumably, forbearances could still be granted in exceptional circumstances, but only if Congress votes that a state of emergency exists and promulgates a set of objectively reproducible tests to govern who does and does not receive capital relief.

Market-Structure Reform. Third, to check the adequacy and credibility of their accounting and capital policies, insurers should be required to test the pricing and risk-management activities in the marketplace. This can be done in two broadly complementary ways.

First, federal insurers should be asked to concern themselves with reinsuring at least some of their coverage with private insurers. Because the value of the full range of their obligations would be hard to appraise, this might entail disaggregating their complete portfolio of guarantee contracts into easy-to-understand packages of homogeneous obligations that could readily be offered for sale in private insurance markets. Conceptually, the contemplated disaggregation and repackaging process parallels the activity of butchers who separate whole chickens into parts and reassemble the pieces as packages of legs, wings, breasts, and backs. The resulting "strips" of homogeneous deposit-insurance coverages could be broken down by account size or account categories or by types, sizes, or locations of the institutions for which reinsurance is being sought. Strips of coverages could be tailored for sale to individual insurance companies or, with appropriate bonding and cross-guarantee provisions, to syndicates of various types of financial institutions. As part and parcel of the constant need to readapt supporting reinsurance documents, market-tested procedures for assuring that government insurers adequately monitor and police insured institutions would develop in an evolutionary way.

Second, federal deposit insurers should be asked to compete freely with one another and with private syndicates for at least some portions of what has been their primary deposit-insurance market. This means allowing institutions (or even depositors) to shift to another insurer whenever they find this to be advantageous for them. Stripping account coverages would make it easier for the government to cut back its basic coverage to an amount much smaller than $100,000. Such a cutback would enhance the potential for depositors to exercise market discipline. It would also permit corporate and household depositors and competitive insurance entities to tailor various forms of less-than-full coverages to fit individual situations.

These market-structure reforms are important because government bureaus are slower to react to implications of technological and environmental change than private institutions are. In a private institution, learning about new processes and products promises to improve profit performance, customer service, and job opportunities for responsive employees. Well-adapted innovative activity tends to improve the lifetime compensation profile an employee can expect, precisely because it will be perceived as benefiting higher officials and stockholders, too. In a government bureau, dealing with new processes and products promises to complicate one's own and one's superiors' jobs without necessarily increasing employee salaries or the bureau's standing accordingly. If government employees want to benefit fully from understanding industry innovations, they must look to opportunities for postgovernment employment.

This weakness in motivation suggests that, in a volatile world, financial risk assessment cannot be left to bureaucrats, no matter how well-trained they might seem for this task. Federal deposit insurers must be made to draw on information created in activities in which the profits of private organizations depend intimately on the accuracy of their continuing analysis of variations in individual institutions' creditworthiness. Private deposit institutions routinely make and act upon their assessment of individual deposit institutions' default risk, for example, in establishing: (1) position limits for bilateral and multilateral clearing arrangements and (2) lists of institutions to which they will and will not sell federal funds. There is little evidence that federal insurers collect or use this information in any systematic way.

Short-run incentive conflicts inherent in government enterprise make it important to develop market-tested procedures for determining when regulatory arrangements are either too tight or too loose. To maintain economic efficiency in an evolutionary environment, it is necessary to establish checks and balances on the exercise of governmental powers. Competition for various portions of a bureau's guarantees, syndicated reinsurance of specific coverages, and opportunities for accountholders to retain varying amounts of risk themselves would generate market signals that bureaucrats could use to do their jobs better.

Improving the Incentive System for Politicians

FSLIC's economic losses in an insolvent client occur long before they are realized in an accounting sense. But FSLIC officially loses money only when it absorbs a client's negative net worth into its own accounts. This leaves politicians far more sensitive to FSLIC's de jure losses and to de jure failures than to FSLIC's de facto losses and client insolvencies.

To better motivate politicians, scapegoating and deniability options created by focusing on de jure failures and expenditures must be narrowed in important ways.

Accounting Reforms. To eliminate the market's need to price the residual nonperformance risk that is inherent in current federal deposit-insurance guarantees, Congress should pass a statute that unambiguously places the full faith and credit of the United States behind the federal deposit-insurance bureaus. But this statute must simultaneously require that annual changes in the market value of deposit-insurance guarantees, and the annual implicit and explicit interest cost of financing these guarantees, be henceforth reported as part of the official budget of the United States. It must no longer be possible for these costs to develop outside of the ordinary process used to control aggregate government spending.

Oversight Reform. Members of Congress should remain free to try to help win reasonable regulatory adjustments for aggrieved constituents. However, Congress as a whole must commit itself to a sterner insolvency-resolution process. Hence, all efforts to win forbearances for individual constituents should be reported to House and Senate ethics and banking committees. These committees should: (1) report publicly each calendar quarter on the amount and character of the aggregate activity that has taken place, and (2) be required to impose sanctions on members who overstep the bounds of appropriate constituent service.

Budget or banking committees should hold hearings each year in which outside experts assess the adequacy of insurers' compliance with the accounting, enforcement, and market-structure requirements described in the previous section.

Improving the Incentive System for Insured Institutions

In a very broad sense, deposit-institution incentives can be reformed in either of two complementary ways, either implicitly by reinforcing market discipline or explicitly by increasing regulatory discipline. Market discipline relies on penalties that the market imposes on managers, stockholders, and uninsured creditors. For regulators, reinforcing market discipline is mainly a matter of making—or at least permitting—timely disclosure of material facts to depositors and other customers who see themselves exposed to loss. As the proviso on customer perceptions makes clear, unless deposit-insurance guarantees are seen to be imperfect or incomplete, this discipline cannot operate at all.

Taking this perspective, several changes in the structure of the deposit-insurance contract may be seen to improve incentives for depositors to monitor and respond to changes in a deposit institution's risk exposure. The conceptually simplest class of adjustments would be either to roll back maximum accountholder coverages or to make enforcement of their limits more credible. Coverage rollbacks can be explicit or implicit. Implicit rollbacks aim at making statutory coverage limitations more credible. This could be accomplished, for example, by enacting a depositor-preference statute or adopting a policy of using modified payoffs for large-bank failures. Explicit rollbacks would alter the terms of deposit-insurance guarantees in one of six ways:

☐ reducing formal coverage limits;
☐ introducing a structure of participating coinsurance that would require depositors to participate in realized losses (with the rate of participation tied, for example, to account size or to the excess of an institution's offering rates on CDs over yields on Treasury securities of similar maturity and liquidity);
☐ incorporating a deductible for losses in excess of some relatively nominal threshold amount;
☐ establishing lifetime limits on the amount an individual can collect from federal deposit insurers (to be monitored by the Internal Revenue Service);
☐ constraining contractually the riskiness of the activities that an insured institution may undertake; or
☐ requiring some forms of deposits to be collateralized by a collection of relatively safe assets.

The purpose of these reforms would be to reduce the completeness of deposit-insurance coverage for depositors that we may presume to be large and sophisticated enough to protect their balances at lower social cost than federal regulators can.

One way in which regulated institutions resist burdensome patterns of regulation is to innovate around them. Given how rapidly financial-services costs and technologies are changing today, the freedom to undertake such innovation holds substantial potential benefits for society as a whole. To maximize those benefits, it is important not to impose costly legal constraints on regulated institutions' ability to enter and exit potentially profitable financial activities and markets. The opportunity costs of complying with regulatory constraints constitute forgone profits that may be interpreted as implicit premiums paid by insured institutions. Authorities' goal should be to keep the restraints on market entry that create these premiums as light as is consistent with maintaining institutional soundness and macroeconomic stability.

As explained in chapter four, taxpayers should want federal officials to maximize FSLIC's value as an economic enterprise. If officials' conflicting incentives could be eliminated, authorities would seek to maximize the capitalized value of net cash flows from premiums, interest on reserves, monitoring costs, and costs incurred in resolving client insolvencies. This would be particularly easy to do if officials could perfectly and costlessly monitor the economic condition of every client and could, without career damage, force the immediate recapitalization of any troubled firm before the economic value of its capital could be exhausted. In these circumstances, a well-run deposit-insurance agency would face no risk of loss and incur no costs. It would need no reserves and would have no need to charge a premium for its services.

This hypothetical case makes it clear that, if we abstract from the incentive problems, the risks to FSLIC come from imperfections in the information and monitoring schemes it operates, and from time lags and other difficulties it encounters in recapitalizing the balance sheets of troubled clients once they are identified as such. In the real world, monitoring, recapitalization, and reserve-management activities undertaken to control and finance losses must be well-designed and the costs they generate must be covered appropriately from implicit and explicit premiums and interest income.

Other things equal, the better the information, monitoring, and recapitalization systems that the insurer operates, the more effectively it can substitute capital requirements for detailed restrictions on the activities of its clients. Given the goal of enforcing timely recapitalization of troubled deposit institutions, several economically valid ways exist to improve each of these systems. Working together, taxpayers, politicians, regulators, and industry representatives have to decide which approach or combination of approaches they prefer.

Emphasizing Market Discipline: Automatic Reassessment of Deposit-Insurance Premiums

When explicit premiums are subject to rebates and supplementary assessments, it is instructive to distinguish between initial premiums (those paid in advance) and subsequent premium adjustments. Rebates and supplementary assessments provide an opportunity for an insurer's clients to reimburse it for the cost of settling the claims that actually pass through to the insurer. Such assessments could be targeted much more selectively than they are now. One approach would be: (1) to require federally insured deposit institutions to be stockholder-owned, and (2) to extend the limited liability of individual deposit-institution stockholders to a multiple of the par value of their shares. Since mutual deposit institutions have been voluntarily converting to stockholder form at a rapid rate during the mid-1980s, the first part of this requirement is probably becoming less burdensome day by day. In the event an institution were to become insolvent, the second provision would make its stockholders personally liable for additional assessments. Extending stockholder liability has the advantage of reducing the basic asymmetry in the distribution of the firm's gains and losses between stockholders and deposit insurers. Extended liability may be conceived as introducing a deductible into deposit-insurance contracts. The market value of this deductible provision to the insurer would increase when and as the economic value of an institution's enterprise-contributed capital declines. Changes in this value would be incorporated in movements into the stock price of each insured institution. For this reason, extended stockholder liability would enhance the role of market discipline for troubled or high-flying firms, while having only a minor impact on the stock value of well-capitalized or conservatively run institutions. The impact ought, in principle, to reflect risks that a firm's operations would otherwise have been able to shift onto its deposit insurer.

Because the value of FSLIC and FDIC rights to demand postfailure or other reimbursements would increase with an institution's leverage and with other kinds of risk exposure, resulting declines in deposit-institution stock prices should be roughly proportional to market ratings of the firm's riskiness. Industrywide, these relative adjustments in deposit-institution stock prices would constitute the transition cost of any market-based type of reform. Extending stockholder liability at insured institutions can be interpreted as a risk-rated increase in the effective insurance premium because its value would depend on the riskiness of the firm. Impounding such a call feature into deposit-institution stock prices would transfer deposit-insurance subsidies back to the taxpayer and change incentives for stockholders, managers, and depositors.

To assure stockholders' willingness and ability to meet their contingent assessments, personal and corporate deposit-institution stockholders could be required to bond their potential liability by placing a sufficiently valuable block of individually owned earning assets in escrow with the deposit institution or some other agent for the insurer. As with margin accounts that guarantee performance in futures trading, the total market value of escrowed assets would be what mattered, not their particular composition. Whenever a stockholder wanted to sell an escrowed asset, he, she, or it would be free to replace that asset with another of like value.

Under existing arrangements, deposit insurers have the right to require stockholders of a troubled deposit institution to contribute additional capital. However, this right (or covenant) loses force as a firm becomes economically insolvent. As a firm's stockholder-contributed capital declines below zero, stockholders lose interest in paying a fee to stop the insurer from taking over the institution. This makes the timing of an insurer's call for additional capital the key to its enforceability. From this perspective, extending stockholder liability may be seen as a way to overcome bureaucratic lags in insurers' monitoring and enforcement subsystems. It would reduce the criticality to insurers of recognizing and responding rapidly to a sudden deterioration in a client's economic condition.

The principal advantage of restoring extended liability for deposit-institution stock is that it would simultaneously lessen the need for explicit regulatory interference in the activities of well-capitalized firms and direct supervisory activity more quickly to troubled institutions. Movements in the stock prices of insured institutions would generate clearer market signals for insurers to use in targeting their monitoring resources. This is because an extension in stockholder liability serves to align stockholder interests more closely with those of federal taxpayers. Today, when an insured firm's enterprise-contributed capital declines, the value of the deposit-insurance guarantees it receives goes up in a nearly offsetting manner. But the value of the call on stockholder resources that this reform would attach to deposit-institution stock would rise to absorb most of the offset. This would mean that go-for-broke speculation by economically insolvent firms need no longer enhance the value of their stock.

To lessen the perceived burdensomeness of abridging stockholder rights, extended liability could be introduced as an optional way of meeting traditional capital requirements. Authorities could offer a lower requirement on paid-in capital for firms whose stock carries the prescribed form of deposit-insurer call on stockholder assets. If capital requirements are to be increased, establishing flexibility in the ways that requirements can be met should prevent stiffer requirements from placing undue burdens on small or conservatively run firms. In small, closely held firms, it should be easy for stockholders to make sure that managers follow policies that keep the value of the call extremely small. At the same time, the insurer would be protected against sudden changes in a client's risk exposure over which it has no control.

Emphasizing Regulatory Discipline: Less-Discretionary Capital Adequacy Requirements

As a general proposition, regulatory discipline will be less burdensome the closer it can be made to mimic the effects of enforceably attaching unlimited liability to deposit-institution stock. The incentives for risk taking that insured institutions face are greatly affected by the information, monitoring, and insolvency prevention/resolution subsystems that their deposit insurer adopts. The information system consists of the accounting principles used to measure client and insurer condition and performance. The monitoring system consists of the techniques the insured uses (e.g., reporting requirements and site examination) to gather this information in timely fashion and to assess the implications of the information collected. The insolvency prevention/resolution or enforcement system consists of the various regulatory measures that the insurer uses to police unfavorable movements in clients' capital or risk exposure that its monitoring uncovers.

As a memory aid, we may think of insurers and deposit institutions as engaged in a long automobile race. Whereas the deposit-institution cars are built to state-of-the-art specifications and maintained carefully, the insurers' cars show disturbing weaknesses in design and maintenance. Insurer windshields (a metaphor for information subsystems) are caked with dirt and grease, making it hard for them to see where they and their rivals are going. Insurer driver seats (i.e., monitoring subsystems) are not firmly secured, making their drivers strain to balance themselves and to process the information the dirty windshields make available. Third, braking, steering, and power controls on insurers' cars (i.e., enforcement subsystems) lack power-boosting and operate with distinct lags. Finally, the method of financing the race and awarding prize money creates an incentive subsystem that offers a much greater range of rewards to daring and skillful deposit-institution drivers and pit crews for each lap they complete than their counterparts on the regulatory team can hope to attain.

The racing car metaphor emphasizes that regulatory discipline is produced by a system of interacting component subsystems. Recognizing what is wrong with the existing system of subsystems is the first step in planning improvements. To improve discipline in a cost-effective manner, we must strengthen the several subsystems in balanced fashion. Along with the need to overcome the political resistance generated by divergent interests, the need for balance is what makes deposit-insurance reform such a tricky business.

Upgrading the Information Subsystem. The keystone of effective reform is developing a clean windshield, i.e., access to meaningful information on client performance and portfolio values. Because GAAP and RAP approve of omitting hard-to-value items and carrying even readily priced assets and liabilities at historical costs, they lend themselves to deceptive use when applied to financial institutions. Authorities should insist on receiving financial statements that convey the information that a well-managed private guarantor would require.

For assessing guarantor risk exposure, RAP and GAAP accounting principles are inferior to market-value accounting, which requires that the carrying value of all assets and nonequity liabilities be marked to their current market values at the end of every accounting period. Market-value accounting further improves on GAAP and RAP by seeking to assign values to every element of what economists call the firm's "extended" balance sheet. Insurers' risk exposure varies with the capitalized value of *all* items capable of contributing positively or negatively to the firm's future income. Thus, insurers should treat the concept of an off-balance-sheet item as a contradiction in terms. Market-value accounting provides a reliable measure of firm performance in volatile times and sets up objective principles for measuring firm capital that are difficult for managers to manipulate with impunity. Market-value accounting requires managers and accountants to engage in deliberate, conscious, and potentially actionable fraud should they want to create the appearances of either profitability or solvency where these conditions do not truly exist.

Difficulties involved in instituting market-value accounting are almost entirely problems of transition. Careful financial analysts regularly attempt to translate a firm's records into market-value terms, and most well-managed financial institutions already employ market-value accounting in internal evaluations of their own performance. While the resulting performance measurements are subject to some degree of inaccuracy, it is crucial to recognize that, on average (and especially for troubled firms), market-value readings provide a more reliable measure of firm strength than either GAAP or RAP does.

As financial innovations have expanded the universe of marketable instruments that are comparable to assets that do not actually trade, the feasibility of market-value accounting has increased correspondingly. Appraisers can: (1) employ prices in secondary markets for comparable instruments; (2) use prices inherent in securitized obligations that are collateralized by cash flows from similar assets; (3) request that information be generated by insurer auctions of hard-to-value assets; (4) utilize the methods that investment bankers use to price takeover bids; and (5) draw on computer models linking movements in loan values to movements in prices of bonds that have similar features or that raise similar valuation issues. Finally, for franchise values and other intangible assets, the task of developing acceptable and objective valuation procedures can be assigned to a self-regulatory board.

Permitting or mandating market-value reports of performance to deposit-institution customers is a relatively low-cost way of improving market discipline on insureds and insurers alike. It would make the existing monitoring and insolvency-prevention systems work more cheaply, more fairly, and more reliably. Recognizing this makes it clear that the strength with which the deposit-institution industry and regulators have resisted market-value accounting has been a major obstacle to effective deposit-insurance reform.

Upgrading the Monitoring Subsystem. I have likened regulators' information subsystem to a racing car's windshield and their monitoring subsystem to the incomplete way in which the regulatory vehicle's driver's seat is installed. The issues in monitoring are how often regulators look through the windshield, whether they use technological opportunities to boost their vision to the 20-20 level, and what sort of problems they keep an eye out for.

Traditionally, agency monitoring efforts have focused on sending teams of field examiners at reasonable intervals to conduct an onsite examination of each client firm's accounts. Except in densely populated regions, agency examiners spend much of their working week on the road in unfamiliar and often hostile environments. Their principal tasks are to review financial statements (often audited ones), to analyze the institutions' earnings and the quality of its loans and investments, and to evaluate the adequacy of the firm's management, liquidity, and capital. The information is pulled together into a formal examination report that points out strengths and weaknesses in the firm's operation. In turn, this narrative report is summarized in a so-called CAMEL rating, which grades institutions on a five-point scale. The acronym CAMEL reflects the main categories of condition and performance on which client institutions are graded: capital; asset quality; management competence and integrity; earnings; and liquidity.

As noted earlier in the book, institutions whose CAMEL rating is 4 or 5 are labeled as "problems" and subjected to more frequent examination and special offsite scrutiny. Offsite monitoring looks at market data, public disclosures, credit ratings assigned by private analysts, and periodic reports filed with various regulators. To a limited extent, offsite analysis is also used as an early warning system to spot institutions that have encountered difficulty since their last examination so that the date of their next examination can be moved up.

Because troubled and aggressively managed institutions often seek to hide their problems from their auditors, customers, and regulators, it is not safe to take institutions' accounts and financial statements at face value. Still, until recently, federal examiners were not specifically asked to examine for fraud.

Another class of monitoring complications concerns the difficulty of measuring the extent to which a deposit institution is exposed to risk through the operations of associated firms. To minimize their net tax and regulatory burden, stockholders have found it advantageous to layer their ownership through holding companies, and to locate activities that are taxed or regulated differentially in a series of carefully structured subsidiary and affiliated corporations. When a subsidiary or affiliated firm runs into trouble, it is hard for regulators to stop the resources of the regulated deposit institution from being used to bail it out. This difficulty makes it inappropriate to analyze the capital and balance sheet of a deposit institution completely independent of those of its related firms. However, the intensity with which deposit insurers needs to monitor and control a client's interaffiliate transactions is a decreasing function of the level and volatility of the firm's contributed capital. It would be sufficient to require prior supervisory approval for a deposit institution's transactions with affiliates and subsidiaries in two types of circumstances: (1) in any calendar quarter in which the institution has lost a specific percentage of its initial capital and (2) whenever the institution's capital ratio has fallen below a designated threshold level. These twin requirements would limit the ability of deposit-institution managers to force the insurer to underwrite losses on activities undertaken in related corporate structures, while minimizing the supervisory burdens that need to be visited on deposit institutions that remain strongly capitalized.

Jurisdictional problems degrade insurers' monitoring processes. The resolution of jurisdictional overlaps has shifted the responsibility for examining important classes of institutions from the insurers who directly bear the risk inherent in client operations to state chartering agencies or to other federal regulators. It has also created blockages in the flow of relevant information among the multiple regulators. The task of minimizing these problems is assigned to coordinating bodies such as the Federal Financial Institutions Examination Council and the Conference of State Bank Supervisors (CSBS).

Financial innovation also complicates the examination process. As the number and scope of problem institutions grew, the size, training, and experience of the field examination force became progressively less adequate. This problem traces both to the vagaries of bureau budget allocations and to bureau or OMB unwillingness to pay high enough salaries or to establish a sufficiently attractive career ladder for examiners to overcome the lifestyle burdens of the job.

The nature of offsite and onsite analysis could be improved in obvious ways. In particular, critics would like to see examiners focus more sharply on fraud detection and make more extensive use of electronic and remote means of analysis. It seems clear that greater emphasis on electronic reporting could reduce the number of weeks the average examiner would have to spend in the field and would diversify examiner activities and raise skill levels in ways that should support higher profiles of career compensation.

Institutions should be permitted to advertise their examination ratings. Examiner performance would benefit from being more directly exposed to public second guessing. Knowing that examiner evaluations could be criticized by outsiders and compared with those of private rating agencies would put pressure on managers of state and federal bureaus to reduce what is now considerable idiosyncratic variation in the quality and character of individual examinations.

Improving the Regulatory Enforcement Subsystem. Historically, industry-wide capital requirements and activity limitations have been the chief instruments of regulatory discipline, but a range of individualized or client-specific policy tools exist. The ultimate in client-specific enforcement action is a declaration of insolvency by the chartering authority, which usually authorizes the insurer to wrest control from existing managers and stockholders. Lesser devices include: agreements of understanding between regulators and individual firms; directives to raise additional capital within a fixed period of time; cease and desist orders; fines levied on officers, directors, and negligent outside auditors; actions to remove particular officers or directors; and proceedings to terminate insurance. All these instruments may be thought of as ways of adjusting deposit-institution cars to make them slower or less maneuverable.

Regulators' rights to use individual tools to tailor adjustments to individual situations are tempered, of course, by legal and political constraints. Client institutions are entitled to due process, which means a right to formal notice, private evidentiary hearings, and subsequent appeals. Deposit-insurance regulators have frequently asked for additional authority to act against failing firms and their officers more readily, to terminate deposit insurance more quickly, and to have depositor (and therefore deposit-insurance) claims against a failed enterprise receive priority in liquidation. Acting under existing authority, regulators have proposed to raise existing capital requirements and to phase in a system of risk-rated capital requirements. Although the burden imposed by these systems is meant to vary with the riskiness of individual institutions, so far no regulator has formally linked its proposals (as economic research would dictate) to estimates of the market value of the guarantee services each institution receives.

The weakness in insurers' proposals and existing subsystems is that they insist on substituting regulators' unreproducible and discretionary judgments for objective market-based measures of what products and services institutions may profitably offer, of what capital is, and of what percentage capital requirements ought to apply to different kinds of balance sheet positions. If they are to eliminate deposit-insurance subsidies to risk taking, capital requirements must vary to absorb increments in the fair market value of the federal guarantees an institution enjoys. To the extent that marginal changes in the value of deposit-insurance services are not offset, an institution's portfolio and operational decisions are distorted. In cases where the effective marginal requirements exceed the fair market value of deposit insurers' guarantee services, the affected business would tend to flow to uninsured institutions and to subsidized activities in which the insured institutions face requirements that are too low.

To regulate capital efficiently, officials must appreciate that the level of deposit-institution capital and the extent of product-line freedoms are not independent issues. In principle, an institution's capital is the discounted present value of the future cash flows that may be projected to accrue to its owners. To make higher capital requirements feasible, it is necessary to leave insured institutions room to shift their product lines as specific profit opportunities wax and wane.

In the 1980s, thrift institutions were not forced into new products and services by legislative fiat. Rather, 1980 and 1982 financial reform acts formally ratified market forces that had made the inherited system of exclusionary rules and portfolio requirements cumulatively more burdensome (Kane 1987b). Changes in the technology of production and delivery of financial services had rendered traditional patterns of specialization insufficiently profitable for many thrift institutions. Efforts to permit customers to transact a wide range of financial services in a single statement framework are importantly restructuring the financial services industry. Front and back offices are becoming increasingly automated and linked together in telecommunication networks, often using facilities that are shared cooperatively with other finanical-services producers. To operate in a cost-efficient manner, modern firms must be permitted to grow: (1) large enough to exhaust economies of large-scale production and distribution; and (2) diverse enough to exploit potential cost savings from jointly producing a broad line of services and offering this menu of services across a firm's base of loyal customers.

One of the great virtues of framing capital requirements as a matter of enforcing a market-value ratio of enterprise-contributed capital is that it would lead authorities to deemphasize burdensome restrictions on thrift-institution product lines. This would permit individual institutions to adapt efficiently to technological changes in financial contracting, data processing, and telecommunications.

The problems raised by regulatory discretion can be clarified by contrasting two alternative proposals for establishing more timely regulatory intervention into the affairs of decapitalized institutions. These proposals were first circulated for comment within a week of each other: by the FHLBB on November 28, 1988 and by the Shadow Financial Regulatory Committee[2] (SFRC) on December 5, 1988.

The FHLBB's proposal focuses on a regulatory measure of capital and embodies a capital-adequacy formula of its own devising. The formula attempts to adapt an approach negotiated in 1988 by U.S. and foreign commercial bank regulators to fit thrift institutions. The formula's purpose is to link an institution's aggregate capital requirement to the degree of risk its operations are thought to pose to

FSLIC. Differential capital-requirement weights are attached to different categories of portfolio positions. The proposed weighting pattern makes the level of required capital (i.e., the threshold for capital adequacy) increase with the extent of an institution's: exposure to interest-rate risk, collateralized borrowing, direct investments, commercial loans, and nonresidential consumer loans. The supporting FHLBB press release estimates that the formula would assign a thrift with "average interest-rate risk" a requirement equal to eight percent of its risk-adjusted assets.

The nature of the regulatory discipline to be visited on institutions that fail to meet these requirements is not fully spelled out, but a minimum acceptable ratio of GAAP capital to total assets is set at 1.5 percent. The hundreds of institutions that fall short of this criterion would be deemed to be in an "unsafe and unsound condition." This test would authorize the FHLBB to require new management and a reorganization of its board of directors and to take "other actions to control the institution." But the FHLBB would leave itself free to decide whether and how much to discipline a decapitalized client on a case-by-case basis.

In contrast, the SFRC proposal seeks to link regulatory discipline to the level of a firm's economic capital and to initiate a sequence of tough disciplinary actions in mandatory and therefore predictable fashion. It defines capital on a market-value basis, as "the difference between the market value of assets and the market value of liabilities other than subordinated debt." It construes assets and liabilities as including off-balance-sheet items and goes on to designate four ranges of capital-to-asset ratios as objective indicators of increasing levels of supervisory concern.

These ranges embody three principal ideas. First, above a clearly adequate capital ratio (tentatively set at 10 percent), only minimal regulatory oversight is required. Second, as an institution's capital falls progressively further below this level, increasingly tough measures of regulatory discipline must be applied and in a predictable way. Third, to minimize insurer losses, a positive capital ratio (which the SFRC fixes at 3 percent) must be designated as so low as to require that a decapitalized institution be either recapitalized or placed into conservatorship immediately. In turn, the conservator would be required to reorganize, merge, sell off, or liquidate the institution within a "short period of time."

The SFRC tentatively designates capital-asset ratios of 6 to 9.9 percent as a range of first-level supervisory concern. In this range, the supervisory authority is required to step up its supervision and to monitor the institution more frequently. As a firm's condition declines through this range, authorities may also require the institution to submit a business plan to restore capital to the fully adequate level within a specified period of time, to suspend dividend payments and unapproved payments to and from affiliated firms, and to restrict asset growth.

If the firm's capital ratio falls in the range of second-level supervisory concern (3 to 5.9 percent), supervision and monitoring become intense. The actions that were discretionary in the previous range become mandatory. Moreover, interest payments on subordinated debt would be stopped and a standby recapitalization plan must be developed for emergency implementation in the event its capital ratio falls below 3 percent.

The SFRC plan conceives of capital as a means of limiting opportunities for stockholders to shift losses to the insurer in the event of liquidation. It treats capital in roughly the same way that commodities exchanges and futures commission merchants treat customer margin accounts on futures contracts. Escalating regulatory discipline as institutions' capital becomes increasingly inadequate loosely mimics a margin call; the 3-percent floor at which recapitalization or reorganization becomes mandatory corresponds to the futures-market practice of selling out the positions of customers who fail to meet a margin-call deadline. Just as futures investors have the option to hold their contracts or accept the proceeds of a sell-off, deposit-institution stockholders would have the right to maintain control by recapitalizing their firms or accepting whatever proceeds devolve from the mandatory reorganization.

Both proposals seek to lessen the effective asymmetry of the risk-sharing mechanism between stockholders and deposit insurers that is established in guaranteeing repayment of the corporation's debt. They propose to do this by demanding that enterprise-contributed capital be kept at an adequate level and by increasing the guarantor's capacity in situations where capital has become inadequate to take over a client's enterprise before its net worth declines to zero.

The difference between the proposals lies in the amount of discretion that politicians and regulators are allowed to exercise. The SFRC scheme allows discretion in setting up the boundaries between different levels of supervisory concern and in the extent to which clients who drift into the first level of concern are subject to regulatory discipline. It also allows for the possibility of establishing a substantial period of transition during which the elements of the SFRC framework would gradually replace the current system.

The critical difference is that the SFRC approach removes three forms of discretionary authority that are central to the FHLBB plan. First, the SFRC defines capital in objective economic terms and requires the insurer to force recapitalization while capital is still positive. Second, it sets the minimum level of capital high enough to protect the deposit-insurance fund from monitoring and regulatory lags. Third, regulatory penalties become mandatory at a level of capital high enough that incentives to engage in go-for-broke gambling are almost certain to be short-circuited.

SUMMARY

I have portrayed federal deposit insurance as a series of formal and informal contracts that obligate and benefit various members of society. The principal parties to these contracts are: taxpayers, elected politicians, deposit-institution regulators, deposit-institution managers and stockholders, and deposit-institution customers. The problem of deposit-insurance reform is to find a way to make the web of contracts incentive-compatible without sacrificing the benefits society intends deposit insurance to deliver. These benefits include: promoting confidence in financial institutions, assuring fair treatment for small depositors, and promoting efficiency in financial intermediation and risk taking.

Although federal deposit insurance worked well enough during its first 30 years, surges in economic volatility during the 1970s and 1980s placed it under increasing strain. This is because the federal deposit-insurance corporations adapted less rapidly and less completely to the changing economic environment than most of the institutions whose deposits they guarantee. Deposit institutions have expanded their aggregate access to subsidies by making obsolete various of the concepts and techniques by which deposit insurers have traditionally tracked, managed, and priced their risk exposure in client operations. FSLIC managers proved particularly slow to perceive (and even slower to counteract) the risk consequences of their clients' cumulative adaptation to change. Because corporate survival and employee jobs would have been on the line, a private guarantor would have innovated more rapidly and more symmetrically to offset the ways in which market developments and nontraditional client activities burdened its own profitability.

The Stubbornness of Subsidies

The various incentive incompatibilities that FSLIC officials have effectively chosen to live with create deposit-insurance subsidies to thrift-institution risk-bearing. These subsidies encourage go-for-broke speculation by decapitalized firms. The predictable result has been a proliferation of zombie thrift institutions. These thrifts may be portrayed as financial terrorists who have carried an unexploded bomb onto a financial-system airplane. Rather than allowing the situation to escalate, it is clearly better for taxpayers to begin to pay the sizable costs of neutralizing the zombies and disarming their bomb.

However, the distributional pattern of deposit-insurance costs and benefits creates winners and losers. Underestimating and hiding the costs helps winners to keep losers from banding together in full force to demand reform. In the case of deposit insurance, the biggest winners are managers and stockholders of high-flying deposit institutions that force deposit insurers into funding their risky plays at subsidized interest rates, and politicians and government officials whose jobs are made more comfortable. Foremost among the losers are those that backstop the insurers: ordinary taxpayers and institutions that compete for business with these high-flying firms. As the product lines of deposit institutions extend into more and more activities, aggrieved competitors increasingly include not only well-managed and well-capitalized deposit institutions but nondepository firms of various kinds—especially insurance companies, securities firms, and real estate companies.

Developing the political will to pay all FSLIC's bills and to reprivatize the government's stake in zombie thrifts is an increasingly pressing short-run problem. A deeper and longer-run problem is to restructure deposit-insurance contracts to eliminate incentive incompatibilities. On any given day, however, neither problem may be said to pose an immediate crisis. Their resolution seems for this reason to be indefinitely postponable.

Defects in contemplated information reporting systems and in related closure options stand out as weak links in reform packages currently being pushed by U.S. authorities. The failure of industry trade associations to focus criticism on these glaring weaknesses testifies to their members' short-sighted concern for postponing transition costs and for preserving near-term subsides even in the face of their firms' growing exposure to loss in a deposit-insurance crisis.

Making Congress Accountable for Backdoor Spending

When the budget deficit is broadly conceived, most of the changes in the unfunded value of deposit-insurance guarantees that we are worrying about today occurred years ago. Policies of covering up and not explicitly financing FSLIC's implicit losses represent an unhealthy type of gambling by politicians and regulators that is encouraged by a crucial defect in the budget discipline under which the federal government operates. This crucial defect consists of focusing budget discipline entirely on explicit (or frontdoor) government receipts and expenditures, while ignoring the impact of the parallel *implicit* (or backdoor) receipts and expenditures that are inherent in changes in the unbudgeted value of federal commitments and guarantees.

The main point of this book is to ask Congress to recognize officially that economists' traditional distinction between *explicit* and *implicit* outlays and receipts implies a parallel distinction between formally budgeted and unbudgeted components of the federal deficit. For years, invisible spending has made the government's *total* deficit much larger than its reported value. The total deficit must take note of net returns on the government's capital stock and changes in the market value of the government's *explicit* and *implicit* debt. Invisible or implicit government debt may be conceived as the expected value of unfunded commitments to provide future government assistance of all sorts. Contractually, these commitments constitute the reverse side of citizen "entitlements" to such items as social security payments and welfare expenditures and of bailouts for politically strong firms and industries.

Losses imbedded in deposit insurance and other guarantee programs deserve to be treated as unbudgeted invisible expenditures precisely because political incentives force Congress and the president to backstop implicitly all federal operations. The comfort given to FSLIC-insured depositors by the presence of the word federal in FSLIC's corporate title is rooted in the perception that, if and when things get tough, losses can be shifted onto federal taxpayers' tab. This is why increased financial weakness of insured deposit institutions may be said to increase the true value of the federal deficit.

Politicians' obsessive concern for minimizing the visible or explicit value of the deficit repeatedly persuaded them to delay needed actions because these would have enlarged the Treasury's *explicit* commitment to the FDIC and FSLIC. Ironically, this unwillingness to formalize what is in the last analysis an unavoidable Treasury commitment has been penny-wise and pound-foolish. It has increased interim customer pressure on the thrift industry and the aggregate value of unfunded FDIC and FSLIC obligations. Deposit-insurance personnel have been made to work unnecessarily close to the edge of an accounting and bureaucratic disaster that could needlessly unravel public confidence in the deposit-insurance system.

In 1988, no candidate for president or for Congress made the need for deposit-insurance reform a major issue in his or her campaign. Nor did the Reagan budget for 1989 embody an adequate program for cleaning up the FSLIC mess. Although George Bush deserves credit for officially reassessing the size of the problem, he has not delivered all the bad news. The most promising way to straighten things out is for taxpayers' elected representatives to tote up the *entire* bill and to pay or finance this bill promptly. More importantly, although no shortage of reform proposals exists, defects in politicians' incentives are not being addressed. Neither President Bush nor any other politician seems ready to propose the restrictive accounting reforms for tracking the future value of backdoor spending through government insurance and guarantee programs that a nation of well-informed and far-sighted taxpayers would require.

Notes

1. This section and some other portions of this chapter draw explicitly on Kane (1987a).

2. The SFRC is modelled on the Shadow Open Market Committee. Composed of eight economists and four lawyers, it meets four times a year to prepare policy statements on current issues in financial regulation.

References

Baebel, Ken, and Edward Golding. 1988. "Management Consignment Comes of Age." *Federal Home Loan Bank Board Journal* 18 (November), pp. 16–19.

Bisenius, Donald J., R. Dan Brumbaugh, Jr., and Ronald C. Rogers. 1986. "Insolvent Thrift Institutions, Agency Issues, and the Management

Consignment Program." Washington: Office of Policy and Economic Research, Federal Home Loan Bank Board (October).

Federal Home Loan Bank Board. 1988. "Loss Prevention Rules Considered for Federally Insured Thrifts." Press Release FHLBB 88-250 (November 28).

Gallagher, Thomas S. 1988. "Rx for the Bank Board's Management Consignment Program." *Issues in Bank Regulation* 11 (Spring), pp. 18–25.

Kane, Edward J. and Chester Foster. 1986. "Valuing Conjectural Guarantees of FNMA Liabilities," in *1986 Proceedings of a Conference on Bank Structure and Competition.* Chicago: Federal Reserve Bank of Chicago, pp. 347–68.

Kane, Edward J. 1987a. "No Room for Weak Links in the Chain of Deposit-Insurance Reform." *Journal of Financial Services Research* 1 (September), pp. 77–111.

———. 1987b. "Adapting Financial Services Regulation to a Changing Economic Environment," in Gary Libecap, ed. *Innovations in New Markets: The Impact of Deregulation on Telecommunications, Airlines and Financial Markets.* Advances in the Study of Entrepreneurship, Innovation and Economic Growth, Vol. 2. Greenwich, Conn.: JAI Press, pp. 223–245.

Shadow Financial Regulatory Committee. 1988. "An Outline of a Program for Deposit Insurance Reform: Exposure Draft." Statement No. 38. Chicago (December 5).

ABOUT THE AUTHOR

Edward J. Kane occupies the Everett D. Reese Chair of Banking and Monetary Economics at Ohio State University. Previously, he taught at Boston College, Princeton University, and Iowa State University. He has held visiting professorships at Istanbul University, Simon Fraser University, and this winter is at Arizona State University's Center for Financial System Research. He has consulted for the Federal Deposit Insurance Corporation, the Federal Home Loan Bank Board, the American Bankers Association, the Department of Housing and Urban Development, various elements of the Federal Reserve System, and the Joint Economic Committee and Office of Technology Assessment of the U.S. Congress.

Professor Kane is a past president of the American Finance Association and a former Guggenheim fellow. In 1981 he won an Ohio State University Alumni Award for Distinguished Teaching. Professor Kane is a Research Associate of the National Bureau of Economic Research and a member of the Shadow Financial Regulatory Committee. From 1975 to 1987 he served as a Trustee and member of the Finance Committee of Teachers Insurance.

Professor Kane received his B.S. degree from Georgetown University in 1957 and his Ph.D. from Massachusetts Institute of Technology in 1960. A widely published author on financial industry and related issues, he serves currently on seven editorial boards. His recent publications include *The Gathering Crisis in Federal Deposit Insurance* (Cambridge, MA: MIT Press, 1985).